This is Egypt...
The Geography
of Egypt

دي مصر...
جغرافية مصر

lingualism

ISBN: 978-1-962752-19-0

Written by Ahmad Al-Masri and Matthew Aldrich

Edited by Hend Khaled and Matthew Aldrich

Audio by Heba Ali

website: www.lingualism.com

email: contact@lingualism.com

TABLE OF CONTENTS

INTRODUCTION

This book is the second in the series دي مصر (This is Egypt...). Book Two, جغرافية مصر (The Geography of Egypt), presents **twelve units**, each exploring a key aspect of Egypt's physical landscape, regions, and natural or human geography, highlighting how they have influenced the country's history, society, and identity.

The texts are written entirely in Egyptian Arabic at an **advanced level** (C1–C2), making them suitable for learners who have studied Lingualism's intermediate-level materials and are ready to push their language skills further. The writing style is clear yet sophisticated, offering learners an authentic challenge while staying accessible with support materials.

Each of the twelve units is built around a central text and is accompanied by:

- **Pre-reading questions** to activate background knowledge and spark curiosity

- **Key vocabulary** drawn from the text to support comprehension

- **Comprehension questions** to check understanding of details and main ideas

- **Discussion and essay prompts** to encourage critical thinking and deeper engagement

- **Professional audio recordings** of each text read by a native speaker from Cairo, to support listening practice and reinforce natural pronunciation and rhythm

Together, these features make the book not only a reading resource but also a complete toolkit for learners aiming to achieve a high level of proficiency in Egyptian Arabic.

HOW TO USE THIS BOOK

This book is designed to help you get the most out of your studies as you advance into the highest levels of Egyptian Arabic. To benefit fully, it's important to approach each unit actively and strategically. The following guide explains the steps you can take to make the most of the materials provided.

Unit Introductions and Pre-Reading Questions

Each unit begins with a short introduction in English. This introduction gives you some background about the subject of the text. Having this context before you begin reading in Arabic helps activate your prior knowledge, set expectations, and make it easier to make educated guesses as you encounter new vocabulary and expressions.

The **Pre-Reading Questions** are designed to get you thinking about the subject. Try answering them in Egyptian Arabic, either by speaking out loud or writing your answers. If you are studying with a tutor or in a class, these questions can spark discussion. If you are studying on your own, they are still valuable to prepare your mind to notice key concepts and vocabulary when you read the text.

Vocabulary Exercise

Each unit highlights **10 Key Vocabulary items** from the text. These are words or phrases you will see in bold within the text (or underlined in a section title). Before reading, you are given their definitions in Arabic—but without the actual words themselves.

Your task is to match each definition to the correct word or phrase from the text. This activity forces you to pay close attention to both the definitions and the surrounding context in the text itself. Use clues from the sentences to help you decide which word matches which definition.

If you are studying with a teacher, you can work together to discuss possible matches before checking the answers. If you are studying alone, try to complete the activity on your own first, then check your answers using the **answer key** at the back of the book.

Approaching the Reading Text

The main text of each unit is a challenging article written in Egyptian Arabic. There is no tashkeel (vowel markings), just as you would see in authentic native materials. This means you must rely on your vocabulary knowledge, grammar skills, and context to determine the correct pronunciation and meaning.

There are many ways you can approach the text. Experiment with different methods to see what works best for you:

- **Listening First**: Play the audio without looking at the text. See how much you can understand by ear alone. Then listen again after studying the text to measure your progress.

- **Reading While Listening**: Follow along in the text while the narrator reads at a natural, native speed. Don't pause—just let yourself absorb as much as you can.

- **Reading Alone**: Read the text without audio, at your own pace. Focus on meaning, guess unknown words from context, and mark phrases you find difficult.

- **Checking with Audio**: Listen again while reading, and this time mark tashkeel only on words you were unsure of. Use the audio as a tool to confirm or correct your guesses.

The English translations are included at the back of the book—not beside the Arabic text. This is intentional. At this level, you should try to understand the text without relying too quickly on translations. Use them only when you are truly stuck.

Using the Audio

The recordings are available as a **free download from our website** and also to **stream on our YouTube channel**. The narrator speaks at a natural, conversational speed—faster than the recordings in our intermediate materials.

This is meant to challenge your listening comprehension at an advanced level. That said, if needed, you can slow down playback on YouTube. You can also repeat short sections of the audio to practice shadowing—reading the text out loud while trying to match the speaker's pronunciation, intonation, and rhythm.

Visit www.lingualism.com/audio, where you can find the free accompanying audio to download or stream (at variable playback rates).

Comprehension Questions

After the text, you will find **10 comprehension questions**. These test your understanding of the details, main ideas, and implications in the text. Try to answer them in Egyptian Arabic if you can.

- **On your own**: Write your answers in a notebook. Check back in the text to confirm, but avoid relying too much on the translation.

- **With a tutor or class**: Discuss your answers aloud. Let the questions guide you back into the text to justify your ideas.

Discussion and Essay Prompts

Finally, each unit includes open-ended questions designed for deeper reflection and critical thinking. These questions are not about right or wrong answers; they are meant to help you **express your opinions and ideas in Arabic**.

If you are studying independently, treat them as writing prompts. Write short essays or journal entries in Egyptian Arabic. If you are studying with a tutor, use them as conversation starters. They are especially useful for building fluency and expressing complex ideas naturally.

Final Tip

There is no single "correct" path through a unit. Some learners may prefer to listen first, then read, while others read first and then listen. What matters most is that you challenge yourself, stay engaged, and make use of the different components—text, audio, vocabulary, and questions—in ways that stretch your abilities while remaining manageable.

Above all, enjoy the journey. As you read about Egypt's landscapes, regions, and environments, you are not only improving your Arabic but also gaining a deeper understanding of the geography that shapes life in Egypt. By the time you complete this book, you will have strengthened your command of Egyptian Arabic and prepared yourself to approach the wider series with confidence, curiosity, and a richer appreciation of both the language and the land.

Bonus Materials: Podcast

Alongside the core content of this book, we are pleased to offer **free bonus materials** for extra listening practice. These are experimental resources created using **AI** to generate podcasts in Egyptian Arabic, each one based on the articles in this book.

In each podcast, two "speakers" discuss the themes and vocabulary of the unit's text in a conversational style. This makes the podcasts a great way to **review and consolidate** what you've learned by hearing familiar words and ideas used in a more natural, interactive setting.

The podcasts are available **only on our YouTube channel** (in the playlist for this book). To keep this strictly a listening activity, no Arabic transcripts are provided. Instead, you'll find **English translations** at the back of the book for support if needed.

While the podcasts sound very authentic, please note that they are **AI-generated** and occasionally contain minor imperfections. For example, you may notice an unusual pronunciation of certain letters, such as ق being pronounced /q/ instead of the common Egyptian /ʔ/, or ث as /th/ instead of /s/ in certain words. On very rare occasions, there may even be small grammar slips. However, each podcast has been carefully **reviewed and approved by a native Egyptian Arabic speaker**, and we believe these resources are not only reliable but also **highly valuable for learners**, precisely because they add a layer of variety and realism.

١

مصر من فوق

When you think of Egypt, the images that often come to mind are the Pyramids, the Nile, or the bustling streets of Cairo. But to truly understand the country, it helps to step back and look at the bigger picture: its geography. Egypt's location at the crossroads of Africa, Asia, and Europe has shaped its history, trade, and culture for thousands of years. Its natural features (the Nile, deserts, mountains, and seas) continue to define how people live and where they settle.

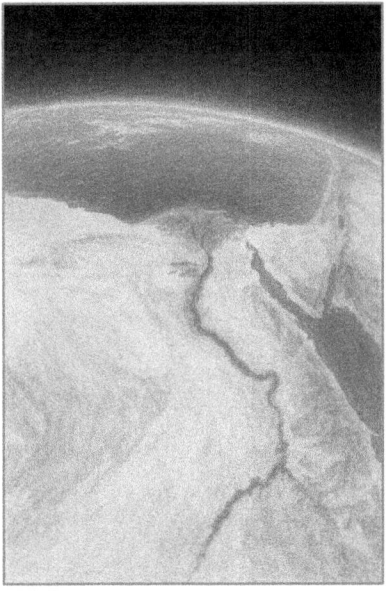

In this unit, we'll take a bird's-eye view of Egypt: where it lies on the map, how its borders and regions are divided, what its climate and terrain look like, and why the Nile remains the lifeline of the nation.

Pre-Reading Questions

١. تفتكر ليه موقع مصر مهم في التاريخ والسياسة والاقتصاد؟

٢. أيه اللي بيميز نهر النيل مقارنةً بغيره من الأنهار في العالم؟

٣. هل شايف إن الحدود الطبيعية أحسن ولا الحدود السياسية في تحديد شخصية البلد؟ ليه؟

Vocabulary

Below are ten definitions. Each one matches a word or phrase that appears in bold in the reading text (or underlined in a section title).

Before reading, try to understand each definition and think of what Arabic term might fit.

Then, as you read, look for the bold words and phrases in the text. Use the surrounding context to help you match them to the definitions.

An answer key is provided at the back of the book.

1. حاجة أساسية الناس ما يقدروش يعيشوا من غيرها

2. خطوط بيرسمها الإنسان باتفاقيات أو قرارات تاريخية

3. شريط ضيق من أراضي خصبة حوالين نهر النيل

4. فواصل زي بحار أو جبال بتحدد شكل بلد

5. لظروف الجوية المعتادة في مكان معيّن على مدى فترة طويلة، زي الحرارة، المطر، والرطوبة

6. مشروع ضخم في أسوان بيخزن الماية ويوفر الكهربا

7. مكان مهم بيأثر على السياسة والتجارة والحروب

8. ممر مائي بيربط البحرين الأحمر والمتوسط، وبيسهّل التجارة

9. منطقة في جنوب مصر معروفة بعاداتها وتقاليدها

10. وحدة إدارية كبيرة في مصر، ليها عاصمة ومحافظ

موقع مصر الجغرافي

مصر موجودة في موقع استراتيجي بيجمع بين تلات قارات: إفريقيا، وآسيا، وأوروبا. بتقع في شمال شرق قارة إفريقيا، وبتمتد على طول الضفة الجنوبية الشرقية للبحر المتوسط. كمان، عندها سواحل طويلة على البحر الأحمر، وده بيديها ميزة بحرية وتجارية كبيرة.

اللي بيميز مصر كمان إنها بتتحكم في واحد من أهم الممرات البحرية في العالم: قناة السويس، اللي بتربط بين البحر المتوسط والبحر الأحمر، وبتسهّل حركة التجارة بين أوروبا وآسيا.

الموقع ده خلا مصر دايمًا في قلب الأحداث، سواء سياسيًا أو اقتصاديًا. من أيام الفراعنة، كانت مصر بوابة بين الشمال والجنوب، والشرق والغرب. والموقع ده فضل له تأثير كبير على تاريخها وثقافتها، وكمان على التحديات اللي بتواجهها. وبجانب أهميته الخارجية، الموقع والجغرافيا نفسهم ليهم دور كبير في شكل التقسيمات الداخلية لمصر، سواء الرسمية أو الشعبية.

الحدود الطبيعية والسياسية والإدارية

الحدود المصرية بتجمع بين العوامل الطبيعية والسياسية. من الشمال، البحر المتوسط بيفصلها عن أوروبا، وده حد طبيعي بيأثر في مناخ المدن الساحلية واقتصادها. من الشرق، البحر الأحمر وشبه جزيرة سينا بيمثلوا حاجز طبيعي بيربط مصر بآسيا عن طريق برزخ السويس.

أما من الجنوب، فالحدود مع السودان سياسية بالأساس، مرسومة في قلب

الصحرا من غير ارتباط بظواهر طبيعية واضحة. نفس الشيء في الغرب، اللي بتمتد فيه حدود مصر مع ليبيا كخط مستقيم طويل وسط الصحرا الغربية.

الحدود الطبيعية زي السواحل أو التضاريس الوعرة ساعدت على تحديد أماكن التجمعات السكانية والمواني، بينما الحدود السياسية كانت نتيجة اتفاقيات وتطورات تاريخية، واتغيرت أكتر من مرة.

على المستوى الإداري، مصر متقسمة رسميًا إلى ٢٧ محافظة، وكل محافظة ليها عاصمة إدارية ومحافظ بيشرف على شؤونها. المحافظات بتنقسم لمراكز ومدن وقرى، وبتختلف في مساحتها وعدد سكانها، وفيه محافظات حضرية مزدحمة زي القاهرة واسكندرية، ومحافظات تانية ريفية أو صحراوية زي الغربية ومطروح.

وبالإضافة للتقسيم الرسمي، فيه تقسيم غير رسمي شائع بين الناس، زي وجه بحري ووجه قبلي، أو مناطق زي الصعيد والدلتا، وهي تقسيمات نابعة من التاريخ والجغرافيا والعادات، وليها تأثير قوي على الهوية المحلية.

المناخ والتضاريس

وبالإضافة لموقعها وحدودها، مصر ليها مناخ بيغلب عليه الطابع الصحراوي الجاف، وده معناه إن أغلب السنة بيكون فيها جو مشمس وأمطار قليلة جدًا. لكن فيه فروق واضحة بين الشمال والجنوب. المدن الساحلية زي إسكندرية ورشيد بيكون الشتا فيها أخف ودرجات الحرارة معتدلة أكتر، خصوصًا بسبب تأثير البحر المتوسط.

أما الجنوب، فدرجات الحرارة أعلى، والجو بيكون جاف أكتر. وفي مناطق زي أسوان أو الأقصر، ممكن توصل الحرارة لفوق الأربعين درجة في الصيف.

التضاريس في مصر متنوعة: وادي النيل، اللي هو شريط ضيق من الأراضي

الخصبة حوالين النهر، بيعيش فيه أغلب سكان مصر. الصحرا الشرقية، بين النيل والبحر الأحمر، والصحرا الغربية اللي بتغطي مساحة ضخمة من أرض مصر. وفي جنوب سينا فيه جبال عالية زي جبل موسى، وعلى ساحل البحر الأحمر فيه سلاسل جبال ممتدة. التنوع ده بيأثر على النشاط الاقتصادي، وأماكن تجمع السكان، وحتى أسلوب حياتهم.

نهر النيل: شريان الحياة

نهر النيل هو القلب النابض لمصر من آلاف السنين. من غيره، كانت مصر هتكون مجرد صحرا شاسعة. النيل بيبدأ رحلته من أعماق أفريقيا، ويمر بعدة دول لحد ما يوصل شمال مصر ويصبّ في البحر المتوسط.

حوالي ٩٥٪ من سكان مصر عايشين على ضفاف النيل، سواء في الوادي أو في دلتا النيل اللي بتبدأ من بعد القاهرة. الدلتا دي منطقة زراعية خصبة جدًا، وبتتزرع فيها محاصيل زي القمح، والرز، والقطن.

النيل مش بس مصدر للماية والزراعة، لكنه كمان وسيلة للنقل والصيد، وعنصر أساسي في الهوية والثقافة المصرية. من أيام الفراعنة، كان النهر محور حياة الناس: يبنوا معابدهم على ضفافه، ينقلوا بضايعهم بالسفن، ويحتفلوا بمواسم فيضانه.

النيل كمان هو اللي بيحدد شكل الحياة الاقتصادية والاجتماعية في مصر. السد العالي في أسوان كان نقطة تحوّل كبيرة في القرن العشرين، لأنه نظم تدفق الماية وقلل من خطر الفيضانات، وكمان وفّر كهربا مائية غيّرت شكل التنمية في الصعيد والدلتا. في نفس الوقت، بناء السد سبّب تغييرات بيئية واجتماعية، زي ترحيل بعض القرى وظهور مشاكل في خصوبة التربة بسبب حجز الطمي. رغم التحديات، السد فضل جزء أساسي من عوامل إدارة الموارد المائية في مصر، وبيمثل رمز لمشروع قومي ضخم غيّر مجرى النهر وحياة الملايين.

ورغم التقدم، النيل لسه هو أساس الحياة في مصر، وأي مشكلة في منابعه أو حصته المائية بتأثر على البلد كلها، وعلشان كده هو دايمًا محور رئيسي في السياسات المائية والخارجية لمصر.

Comprehension Questions

1. أيه اللي بيميز موقع مصر الجغرافي؟

2. ليه قناة السويس مهمة لمصر والعالم؟

3. أيه الفرق بين الحدود الطبيعية والسياسية؟ هات أمثلة من النص.

4. مصر متقسمة رسميًا لأيه؟ وكام محافظة فيها؟

5. أيه الفرق بين التقسيم الرسمي وغير الرسمي (زي الصعيد والدلتا)؟

6. أيه طبيعة المناخ في مصر؟ وأيه الاختلاف بين الشمال والجنوب؟

7. ليه أغلب سكان مصر عايشين حوالين النيل؟

8. أيه أهم المحاصيل اللي بتتزرع في دلتا النيل؟

9. إزاي السد العالي غيّر الحياة في مصر؟

10. ليه نهر النيل لسه بيمثل محور مهم في السياسات المصرية لحد دلوقتي؟

Discussion / Essay Prompts

1. هل تعتقد إن موقع مصر ميزة أكتر ولا تحدي أكبر؟ وضّح.

2. إزاي ممكن مصر تتعامل مع المشاكل المرتبطة بالمناخ الصحراوي أو ندرة الماية؟

3. هل السد العالي كان ليه فوائد ولا أضرار أكتر؟ ناقش.

٢
النيل والمجتمع

For thousands of years, Egyptian life has revolved around the Nile. It is not just a river but the foundation of agriculture, transport, settlement, and culture. The fertile valley and delta support most of Egypt's population, even though they make up only a small fraction of the country's total land area.

In this unit, we'll look at how the Nile has shaped Egyptian society, from farming practices and transportation to modern developments like the Aswan High Dam. The river remains both a source of opportunity and a challenge, linking the past with the present in Egypt's ongoing story.

Pre-Reading Questions

١. تفتكر ليه أغلب المصريين ساكنين حوالين نهر النيل مش في الصحرا؟

٢. أيه أهمية الزراعة في حياة المصريين زمان ودلوقتي؟

٣. هل سمعت قبل كده عن السد العالي؟ تفتكر كان أيه تأثيره؟

Vocabulary

Read the definitions below. Each one matches a bold word or phrase in the text. Try to guess the terms first, then find them in context as you read. Answers are at the back of the book.

1. استخدام النيل كوسيلة لنقل الناس أو البضايع

2. التوسع في البناء على حساب الأراضي الزراعية

3. الرواسب اللي بيجيبها النيل مع الفيضان وبتخصّب الأرض

4. بحيرة صناعية اتكوّنت ورا السد العالي

5. بنايات ضخمة على مجرى النهر علشان تخزن وتتحكم في الماية

6. زيادة نسبة الأملاح اللي بتأثر على خصوبة الأرض

7. عمل كبير بيوحد الناس وبيمثل إنجاز للبلد كلها

8. منطقة مثلثة خصبة شمال مصر، بين فرعين دمياط ورشيد

9. مواد كيماوية بيستخدمها المزارعين لزيادة إنتاج الأرض

10. نظام حديث لرش الماية على الأراضي الزراعية

الدلتا والوادي

من أول ما تدخل مصر، بتلاحظ إن أغلب الناس ساكنين على شريط ضيق حوالين نهر النيل. المنطقة دي اسمها "الوادي"، ودي من أخصب الأراضي في مصر.

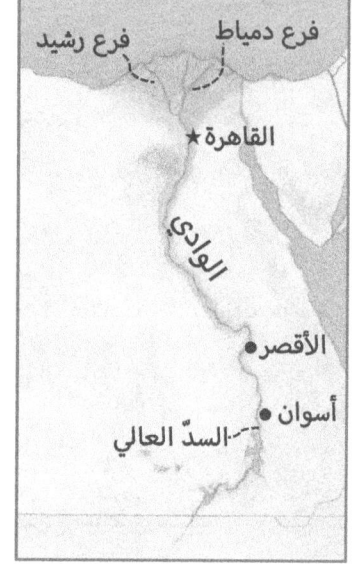

الوادي بيمتد من أسوان في الجنوب لحد القاهرة، وبعدها النيل بيتفرّع شمالًا في شكل مثلث كبير اسمه "دلتا النيل"، بين فرعين دمياط ورشيد.

الوادي والدلتا هما قلب مصر النابض. رغم إنهم بيشكّلوا أقل من ٥٪ من مساحة مصر الكلية، إلا إن أكتر من ٩٠٪ من السكان عايشين فيهم. السبب بسيط: التربة خصبة، والماية قريبة، والظروف مناسبة للزراعة.

الدلتا منطقة زراعية من الطراز الأول، وفيها قرى كتير وشبكات ري وتصريف متطورة نسبيًا. لكن كمان بتواجه تحديات كبيرة: الزحف العمراني اللي بياكل الأراضي الزراعية، والتلوث، ومشكلة ملوحة التربة في بعض المناطق بسبب قُربها من البحر.

أما الوادي، فبيضم مدن كبيرة زي الأقصر وأسوان وقنا والمنيا. زمان، كانت قرى الوادي بتعتمد بشكل كامل على النيل في الشرب والزراعة والصيد. لكن دلوقتي، مع التوسع الحضري والتغيرات المناخية، فيه ضغط كبير على الموارد المائية.

الزراعة والنقل على النيل

النيل مش بس نهر، ده شريان بيغذي الزراعة والنقل والحياة اليومية. من زمان، والمصريين بيعتمدوا عليه في زراعة المحاصيل الأساسية زي القمح، والرز،

والدرة، والقطن. الأراضي اللي حوالين النهر بتتميز بخصوبة عالية بسبب ترسيب الطمي اللي بييجي مع ماية الفيضان (قبل بناء السد العالي).

الري التقليدي كان بيعتمد على السواقي والترع، لكن دلوقتي فيه نظم حديثة زي الري بالرش والتنقيط، وده مهم في ظل نقص الماية. الدولة كمان بتحاول تطوّر نظم الزراعة علشان توفّر الماية وتحافظ على الإنتاج.

أما من ناحية النقل، فالنيل كان دايمًا وسيلة فعالة وآمنة لنقل الناس والبضايع. لحد النهارده، لسه فيه مراكب نيلية بتتنقل بين المدن، خصوصًا في الجنوب، وكمان فيه سفن سياحية بتتنقل السياح بين الأقصر وأسوان.

لكن النقل النهري بقى أقل انتشارًا من زمان، بسبب تطور الطرق والكباري وشبكات القطارات. ورغم كده، فيه جهود لإحياء النقل النهري لتقليل الزحمة على الطرق، وتقليل التلوث.

المزارعين والصيادين بيعتمدوا على النيل بشكل مباشر، لكن كمان كل بيت في مصر بيتأثر بطريقة غير مباشرة: في الأكل، في الأسعار، وفي توفر الماية. علشان كده، أي تهديد للنيل، سواء داخلي أو خارجي، بيكون له تأثير على المجتمع كله.

السد العالي وتأثيره

في الستينات، دخلت مصر مشروع ضخم: بناء السد العالي في أسوان. الهدف كان واضح: السيطرة على فيضان النيل، وتخزين الماية، وتوليد الكهربا. المشروع ده غيّر شكل العلاقة بين المصريين والنهر بشكل جذري.

قبل السد، كان النيل يغمر الأراضي في موسم الفيضان، وده كان بيساعد في تجديد خصوبة التربة، لكنه كان كمان بيسبب مشاكل، خصوصًا لو الفيضان كان عنيف. بعد بناء السد، بقى فيه تحكم كامل في الماية، وقدرت الدولة تنظم

الري على مدار السنة.

السد العالي كمان بيوفّر كهربا لجزء كبير من مصر، وكان نقلة مهمة في التنمية الصناعية. وكمان أنشأ بحيرة ناصر، اللي بتمتد لمئات الكيلومترات، وبتخزن كميات ضخمة من الماية.

لكن رغم الفوائد، في كمان آثار سلبية. غياب الطمي اللي كان بييجي مع الفيضان أدى إلى نقص خصوبة التربة، واحتاج المزارعين يستخدموا أسمدة صناعية أكتر. كمان، بعض أنواع الأسماك قلت، والنظام البيئي اتأثر.

السيطرة على النيل خلّت الدولة تتحمل مسؤولية أكبر في إدارة المياه. ومع زيادة السكان، زادت التحديات. وفي العقود الأخيرة، ابتدت مصر تواجه أزمات مائية بسبب مشروعات سدود في دول منبع النيل، خصوصًا في إثيوبيا.

ورغم كل ده، بيفضل السد العالي رمز لمشروع قومي ناجح، وواحد من أهم الإنجازات في تاريخ مصر الحديث. بيجمع بين الفخر الوطني والتحديات اللي بتتطلب حلول مستمرة.

Comprehension Questions

1. أيه الفرق بين الوادي والدلتا؟ وليه أغلب السكان عايشين فيهم؟

2. أيه أهم التحديات اللي بتواجه الدلتا دلوقتي؟

3. أيه المحاصيل الأساسية اللي بتتزرع حوالين النيل؟

4. إزاي اتغيرت نظم الري من زمان لدلوقتي؟

5. ليه النقل النهري قل عن زمان؟

6. السد العالي اتبنى ليه؟ وأيه الفوايد اللي حققها؟

7. أيه الآثار السلبية لبناء السد العالي على التربة والزراعة؟

8. أيه العلاقة بين السد العالي وتوليد الكهربا؟

9. أيه التهديدات اللي بتمثلها مشروعات سدود دول المنبع لمصر؟

10. ليه السد العالي لسه رمز مهم في تاريخ مصر؟

Discussion / Essay Prompts

11. هل تعتقد إن مصر معتمدة زيادة على النيل؟ إزاي ممكن تقلل الاعتماد ده؟

12. إزاي ممكن الدولة تحافظ على الأراضي الزراعية في الدلتا؟

13. لو كان النيل مش بيعدي في مصر، كان شكل البلد هيبقى أيه؟

٣

الصحرا مش بس رملة

When most people imagine Egypt, the desert often comes to mind—endless stretches of sand under the blazing sun. But Egypt's deserts are far more diverse and surprising than that simple picture. Covering the majority of the country's  land area, the Eastern and Western Deserts contain mountains, caves, oases, wildlife, and even sites of major battles.

In this unit, you'll explore how the desert has shaped Egypt's geography, history, and modern development. From ancient trade routes and mineral wealth to today's solar energy projects and eco-tourism, the desert continues to play a vital role in Egypt's past, present, and future.

Pre-Reading Questions

1. أيه الصورة الذهنية اللي بتيجي في بالك لما تسمع كلمة "صحرا"؟

2. هل تعتقد إن الصحرا ممكن يكون ليها فوايد اقتصادية أو سياحية؟

3. سمعت قبل كده عن واحة سيوة أو العلمين؟ تعرف أيه عنهم؟

Vocabulary

Read the definitions below. Each one matches a bold word or phrase in the text. Try to guess the terms first, then find them in context as you read. Answers are at the back of the book.

1. الطريقة المعتادة اللي بيعيش بيها الناس، من عادات، أنشطة، وروتين يومي

2. تكوين جيولوجي نادر في الصحرا الغربية

3. قبائل بدوية عايشة في الصحرا الشرقية

4. ماية موجودة تحت الأرض في العيون والآبار

5. مشروعات بتستغل الموارد بشكل يحافظ عليها للمستقبل

6. مناطق خضرا في نص الصحرا فيها ماية وزراعة

7. منطقة ضخمة من الكثبان الرملية في الصحرا الغربية

8. منطقة محمية علشان تحافظ على النباتات والحيوانات

9. موقع أثري في واحة سيوة من العصر الفرعوني

10. نوع سياحة بيركز على الطبيعة والهدوء وحماية البيئة

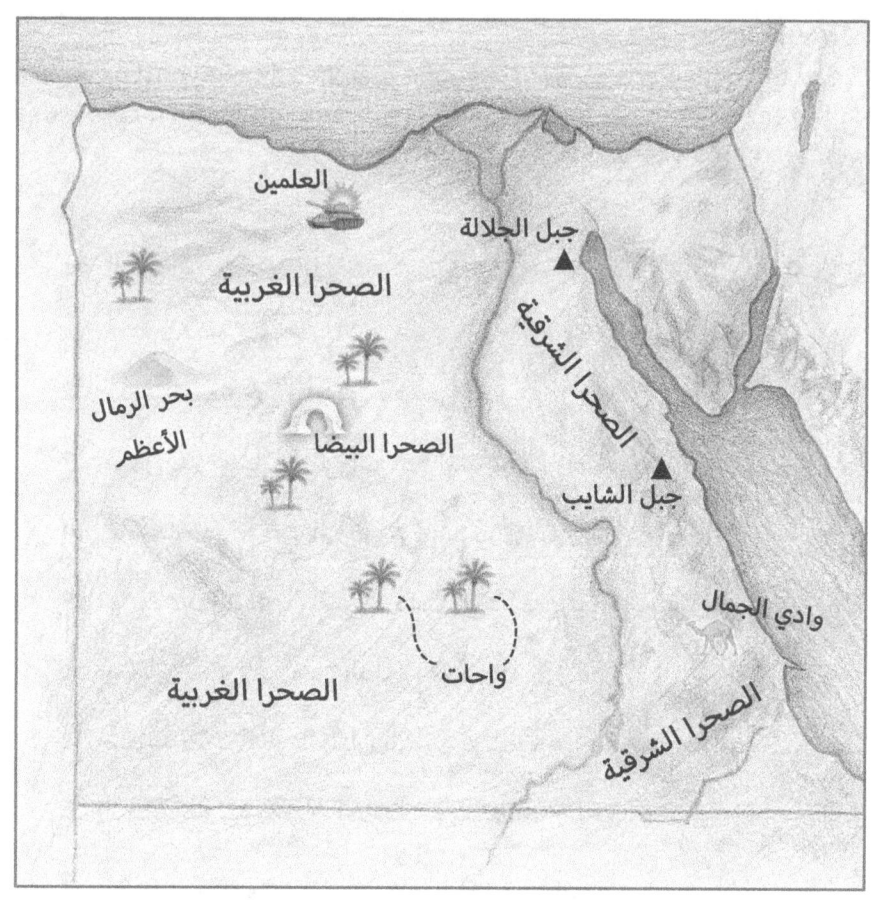

الصحرا الغربية

الصحرا الغربية بتغطي حوالي تلتين مساحة مصر، وبتفصل وادي النيل عن حدود ليبيا. ورغم إن كلمة "صحرا" بتخلينا نتخيل أرض قاحلة، لكنها في الحقيقة مليانة تنوع جيولوجي وجغرافي. فيها سلاسل جبال، وكثبان رملية ضخمة، وواحات خضرا وسط اللون الأصفر الدهبي.

أشهر جزء فيها هو بحر الرمال الأعظم، اللي بيضم واحدة من أكبر الكثبان الرملية في العالم، وده بيجذب المغامرين ومحبي التخييم. كمان فيها مناطق صخرية فيها تكوينات جيولوجية نادرة، زي الجبل الكريستالي، والصحرا

البيضا اللي متغطية بصخور كلسية ناصعة البياض، شكلها زي ماتكون من عالم تاني.

الصحرا الغربية كمان كانت مسرح لأحداث تاريخية مهمة، خصوصًا في الحرب العالمية التانية، لما حصلت معارك بين قوات الحلفاء والمحور في منطقة العلمين.

النهارده، الدولة بتحاول تستفيد من مساحة الصحرا الواسعة دي، من خلال مشروعات زراعية وسكنية، وزيادة الاعتماد على الطاقة الشمسية. ومع التوسع في البنية التحتية، بدأت تظهر طرق جديدة بتربط الصحرا بالدلتا والوادي، وبتسهّل الحركة والاستثمار.

الصحرا الشرقية

الصحرا الشرقية أقل شهرة من الغربية، لكنها مش أقل أهمية. بتمتد بين وادي النيل والبحر الأحمر، ومساحتها حوالي ٢٢٪ من مساحة مصر. فيها تضاريس وعرة أكتر من الغربية، وجبال عالية بتفصلها عن الساحل، زي جبل الشايب وجبل الجلالة.

الصحرا دي غنية جدًا بالمعادن. من أيام الفراعنة، كانت مصدر للدهب والنحاس والحجر الجيري، ولسه لحد النهارده فيها مناجم شغالة، ومناطق استكشاف جديدة. وبتعتبر كمان بوابة للمواني على البحر الأحمر، زي سفاجا والقصير، ودي أماكن حيوية للتجارة الدولية.

فيها محميات طبيعية زي وادي الجمال، اللي بيضم حياة برية متنوعة من نباتات، وغزلان، وطيور نادرة. المنطقة دي كمان بتشهد وجود قبائل بدوية زي العبابدة

والبشارية، اللي لسه محافظين على تقاليدهم وأسلوب حياتهم رغم التطور.

الدولة بتشتغل على تطوير الصحرا الشرقية من خلال إنشاء مناطق صناعية، وتوسيع شبكة الطرق، وربط المدن الساحلية بصعيد مصر، وده بيعزز دورها الاقتصادي والاستراتيجي.

واحات مصر

وسط الامتداد الصحراوي الكبير في مصر، بتظهر الواحات كجواهر خضرا بتكسر رتابة الرمال. أشهر الواحات هي سيوة، والواحات البحرية، والداخلة، والخارجة، والفرافرة. كل واحة ليها طابع خاص، وتاريخ مميز، ومجتمع محلي ليه عادات مختلفة.

واحة سيوة مثلًا مشهورة بتراثها الأمازيغي، وبلغتها المميزة، ومياتها الكبريتية، وجمال طبيعتها. فيها معالم تاريخية زي معبد آمون، و"جبل الموتى".

الواحات مش بس مناطق زراعية، لكن كمان مراكز حضارية فيها بيوت تقليدية، وأسواق، ومدارس، ومراكز صحية. السكان بيزرعوا نخيل، وزتون، وخضروات، وبيعتمدوا على المياه الجوفية من العيون والآبار.

في السنوات الأخيرة، بقت الواحات مقصد مهم للسياحة البيئية والعلاجية، بسبب جوها النقي، وينابيعها الطبيعية، والهدوء اللي بتقدمه بعيد عن زحمة المدن. كمان فيها فرص استثمارية كبيرة في الزراعة المستدامة والطاقة الشمسية.

لكن في نفس الوقت، فيه تحديات زي نقص المياه، وتغير المناخ، والهجرة من الواحات للمدن الكبرى، ودي بتأثر على الاستقرار السكاني والاقتصادي في المناطق دي.

الحياة في الصحرا

الحياة في الصحرا مش سهلة، لكن برضو مش مستحيلة. فيه مجتمعات بدوية عاشت فيها قرون، واتعلمت تتأقلم مع الظروف القاسية. البدو بيعتمدوا على التنقل، وتربية الجمال والمِعيز، واستخدام الموارد الطبيعية بذكاء.

النهارده، نمط الحياة في الصحرا بدأ يتغير. فيه قرى حديثة بتتبني، وطرق بتتوصل، وخدمات بتوصل للناس اللي كانوا معزولين لفترة طويلة. المدارس والمراكز الطبية بقت موجودة حتى في أماكن بعيدة.

لكن لسه فيه مشاكل: العزلة، قلة فرص العمل، ومحدودية الموارد. ومع تغير المناخ، بقت بعض المناطق أكتر عرضة للجفاف. في نفس الوقت، ناس كتير من سكان الصحرا بيهاجروا للمدن يدوروا على فرص أفضل، وده بيهدد الثقافات المحلية القديمة بالاختفاء.

رغم كده، الصحاري المصرية فيها فرص عظيمة للتنمية المستدامة، سواء في السياحة البيئية، أو الطاقة المتجددة، أو الزراعة الحديثة. ومع التخطيط السليم، ممكن تتحول من مناطق مهمّشة لمراكز حيوية لمستقبل مصر.

الحياة في الصحرا بتعلّم الصبر، والاعتماد على النفس، وقيمة البساطة. ودي قيم ممكن تكون مهمة جدًا في زمن السرعة والتكنولوجيا اللي عايشينه دلوقتي.

Comprehension Questions

1. أيه اللي بيميز الصحرا الغربية عن الصحرا الشرقية؟

2. ليه منطقة العلمين مهمة في التاريخ؟

3. أيه أهم الموارد الطبيعية الموجودة في الصحرا الشرقية؟

4. أيه بعض الأمثلة للمحميات الطبيعية اللي موجودة في الصحرا؟

5. أيه أشهر الواحات في مصر؟ وكل واحة بتمتاز بأيه؟

6. إزاي الواحات بتجمع بين الزراعة والخدمات المجتمعية؟

7. ليه بقت الواحات مقصد مهم للسياحة في الفترة الأخيرة؟

8. أيه التحديات اللي بتواجه الحياة في الواحات؟

9. إزاي نمط حياة البدو بيساعدهم يتأقلموا مع الظروف الصحراوية؟

10. في رأيك، أيه الفرص اللي ممكن تقدمها الصحاري المصرية لمستقبل مصر؟

Discussion / Essay Prompts

1. في رأيك، هل حياة البدو ممكن تستمر زي ما هي في العصر الحديث؟ ليه أو ليه لأ؟

2. أيه رأيك في فكرة السياحة البيئية في الواحات: فرصة اقتصادية ولا تهديد للبيئة؟

3. لو كنت هتعيش في مكان في الصحرا، تختار واحة ولا مدينة جديدة؟ وليه؟

٤
البحار والسواحل

Egypt is often thought of as a land of the Nile, but its long coastlines on the Mediterranean and Red Seas are just as important. For thousands of years, these waters have connected Egypt to the wider world through trade, migration, and cultural exchange. Coastal cities like Alexandria and Port Said became gateways where Egypt met Europe, Africa, and Asia.

In this unit, you'll discover how the seas and coasts influence Egypt's climate, economy, and daily life. Fishing, shipping, tourism, and energy projects all depend on the sea, while coastal communities balance tradition and modern development.

Pre-Reading Questions

١. هل زرت كده مدينة ساحلية في مصر؟ أيه أوجه إختلافها عن المدن الداخلية؟

٢. في رأيك، أيه المخاطر اللي ممكن تواجه السواحل بسبب السياحة أو العمران؟

٣. تتوقع أيه الفرق بين البحر المتوسط والبحر الأحمر من حيث الطبيعة والأنشطة؟

Vocabulary

Read the definitions below. Each one matches a bold word or phrase in the text. Try to guess the terms first, then find them in context as you read. Answers are at the back of the book.

1. أوقات معينة في السنة بتكون مناسبة لصيد أنواع معينة من السمك

2. بناء مدن ومنتجعات وقرى جديدة على السواحل

3. تبادل بضايع ونقلها عن طريق البحر والمواني

4. تكوينات بحرية ملونة بتعيش فيها أنواع كتيرة من الكائنات

5. جو مش شديد الحرارة ولا البرودة، مناسب للزراعة والسياحة

6. شغل قديم بيتوارثه الناس جيل ورا جيل زي الصيد

7. مدينة على البحر الأحمر مشهورة بالسياحة والشعاب المرجانية

8. مرافئ مخصصة لاستقبال اليخوت والسفن السياحية

9. مواد ضارة بتدخل البحر وتضر الكائنات البحرية وصحة الناس

10. نشاط سياحي ورياضي لاكتشاف أعماق البحر والشعاب المرجانية

ساحل البحر المتوسط

الساحل الشمالي لمصر بيطل على البحر المتوسط، وبيمتد من حدود رفح في الشرق لحد السلوم في الغرب، بطول حوالي ١٠٠٠ كيلومتر. المنطقة دي كانت دايمًا ليها أهمية استراتيجية وتاريخية كبيرة. مدن زي إسكندرية، بورسعيد، ودمياط مش بس مواني، لكنها كمان مراكز ثقافية وتجارية مهمة.

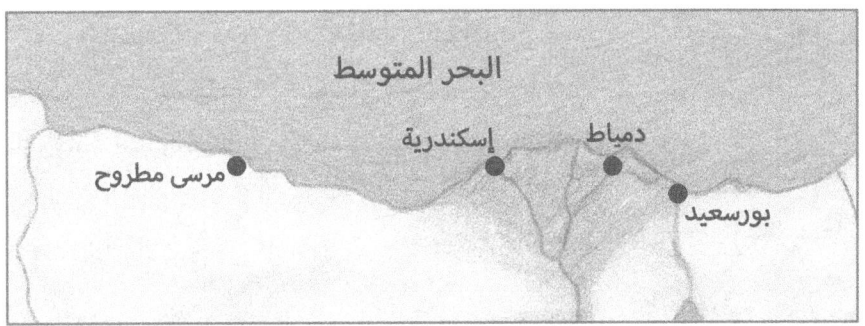

إسكندرية بالذات ليها مكانة خاصة؛ من أيام الإغريق لحد النهارده، دايمًا كانت مدينة بتجمع بين الشرق والغرب. فيها واحد من أكبر المواني في مصر، وكمان مشهورة بجامعتها ومكتبتها العالمية.

المناخ المعتدل، والرطوبة النسبية، بيخلوا الساحل الشمالي مكان مناسب للزراعة، خصوصًا زراعة الزيتون والتين. كمان بقى من أهم المقاصد السياحية، خصوصًا في الصيف، لما آلاف المصريين بيروحوا يصيفوا في المدن الساحلية والقرى السياحية.

لكن في السنين الأخيرة، زاد الاهتمام بالتنمية العمرانية على الساحل، وده أثار جدل حوالين التأثير على البيئة الساحلية، والتوازن بين الاستثمار والحفاظ على الطبيعة.

ساحل البحر الأحمر

الساحل الشرقي لمصر بيطل على البحر الأحمر، وبيمتد من السويس في الشمال لحد حلايب وشلاتين في الجنوب. المنطقة دي أقل كثافة سكانية من الساحل الشمالي، لكنها بقت من أهم المناطق السياحية في مصر والعالم.

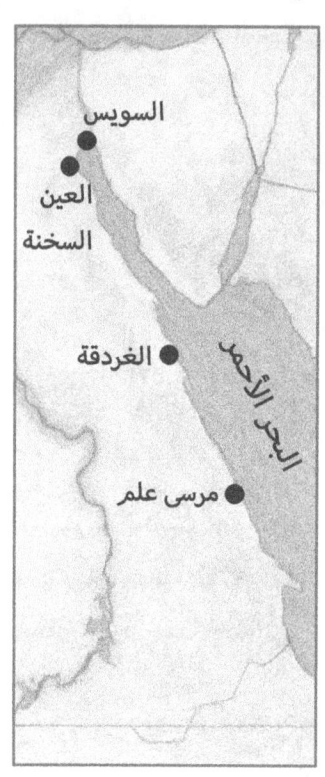

مدن زي الغردقة، مرسى علم، والعين السخنة بقت معروفة عالميًّا بجمال شواطئها، وشعابها المرجانية النادرة، ومايتها الصافية. البحر الأحمر من أغنى البحار بالتنوع البيولوجي، وده بيجذب الغطاسين والسياح من كل حتة.

كمان في مواني مهمة زي سفاجا والسويس، اللي بتخدم التجارة مع الخليج وآسيا. والموقع القريب من قناة السويس بيخلّي الساحل ده عنصر مهم في الاقتصاد المصري.

فيه كمان مشاريع كبيرة للطاقة الشمسية وطاقة الرياح بتتطور في المنطقة دي، علشان تستفيد من الموارد الطبيعية، وتدعم التحول للطاقة المتجددة.

رغم الجمال والفرص، فيه تحديات برضو، زي التأثير البيئي للأنشطة السياحية، ومشكلة الحفاظ على الشعب المرجانية في مواجهة التغير المناخي.

الصيد، التجارة، والسياحة البحرية

البحرين – المتوسط والأحمر – مش بس حدود مائية لمصر، لكنهم مصدر حياة وفرص اقتصادية. الصيد مثلاً مهنة تقليدية في مجتمعات كتير على السواحل، خصوصًا في رشيد، دمياط، السويس، وسفاجا.

حياة الصيادين بتعتمد على مواسم الصيد، ونوع الأسماك، والطقس. في بعض المناطق، فيه تقنيات تقليدية لسه مستخدمة، وفي مناطق تانية، بدأ يظهر صيد حديث بمعدات متطورة.

التجارة البحرية عنصر أساسي في الاقتصاد. قناة السويس مثلاً بتربط بين البحرين، وبتوفر دخل كبير لمصر من رسوم المرور. كمان فيه مواني كبيرة زي إسكندرية، بورسعيد، والسويس، بتستقبل سفن من كل أنحاء العالم، وبتسهم في حركة الصادرات والواردات.

السياحة البحرية بقت مجال واعد. مش بس بسبب الغوص والشواطئ، لكن كمان في الرحلات البحرية، والمواني السياحية اللي بتستقبل اليخوت والسفن السياحية.

فيه اهتمام متزايد بتطوير البنية التحتية الساحلية: مرافئ، منتجعات، وكورنيشات. لكن مع كل ده، لازم يكون فيه وعي بيئي علشان نحافظ على البحرين ونمنع التلوث البحري، اللي ممكن يأثر على الحياة البحرية وصحة الإنسان.

البحرين كانوا دايمًا مصدر إلهام للمصريين، من قصص الصيادين للأغاني الشعبية، ومن التراث الفرعوني للواقع الحديث. والنهارده، مستقبلهم مرتبط بتخطيط ذكي بيوازن بين التنمية والحفاظ على البيئة.

Comprehension Questions

1. أيه البحر اللي بيطل عليه الساحل الشمالي؟ وبيمتد منين لفين؟

2. ليه مدينة إسكندرية ليها مكانة خاصة تاريخيًا وثقافيًا؟

3. أيه المحاصيل اللي بتتزرع في الساحل الشمالي بسبب مناخ المنطقة؟

4. ليه الساحل الشمالي بقى مقصد سياحي مهم في الصيف؟

5. أيه المدن الرئيسية اللي موجودة على ساحل البحر الأحمر؟

6. ليه البحر الأحمر مشهور على مستوى العالم؟

7. أيه المشاريع الجديدة اللي بتتطور في منطقة البحر الأحمر لدعم الطاقة المتجددة؟

8. أيه التحديات البيئية اللي بتهدد الشعب المرجانية؟

9. أيه دور قناة السويس في التجارة البحرية؟

10. ليه لازم يكون في وعي بيئي مع تطوير البنية التحتية الساحلية؟

Discussion / Essay Prompts

1. إزاي ممكن نوازن بين الصيد التقليدي والصيد الحديث؟

2. هل تحب تعيش في مدينة ساحلية؟ ليه أو ليه لأ؟

3. أيه رأيك في السياحة البحرية: فرصة اقتصادية لمصر ولا تهديد للبيئة البحرية؟

O
القاهرة الكبرى

Cairo has stood for more than a thousand years as a crossroads of history, culture, and daily life. From the first mosques of Fustat to the

grand boulevards of Khedive Ismail, the city has expanded into a vast urban sprawl that now includes Giza and Qalyubia. Greater Cairo is a place of striking contrasts— monuments beside high-rises, bustling streets next to quiet neighborhoods, ancient heritage layered with modern change. In this unit, you'll explore how Cairo became the beating heart of Egypt, and what makes life there unlike anywhere else.

Pre-Reading Questions

١. ليه دايمًا القاهرة ليها مكانة خاصة في تاريخ مصر؟

٢. أيه المشاكل اللي ممكن تحصل لما عدد السكان يزيد بسرعة في مدينة كبيرة؟

٣. هل شايف إن العاصمة الإدارية الجديدة هتقدر تخفف الضغط عن القاهرة؟

Vocabulary

Read the definitions below. Each one matches a bold word or phrase in the text. Try to guess the terms first, then find them in context as you read. Answers are at the back of the book.

١. أول مدينة إسلامية في مصر بناها عمرو بن العاص سنة ٦٤٢م

٢. الجزء التاريخي اللي أسسه الفاطميين وفيه الأزهر والمعالم الإسلامية

٣. تكدّس كبير للناس أو العربيات في الشوارع أو الأماكن العامة، وده بيخلي الحركة بطيئة وصعبة

٤. حاكم مصري في القرن الـ ١٩ حاول يطوّر القاهرة على الطراز الأوروبي

٥. مؤسسة ثقافية بتقدم عروض موسيقية ومسرحية

٦. مدينة صناعية كبيرة في القليوبية، جزء من القاهرة الكبرى

٧. مشروع ضخم شرق القاهرة هدفه يخفف الضغط السكاني والإداري

٨. من أقدم وأكبر الجامعات في مصر

٩. مناطق سكنية اتبنت من غير تخطيط رسمي أو خدمات كافية

١٠. منطقة سكنية جديدة اتبنت لنقل سكان العشوائيات

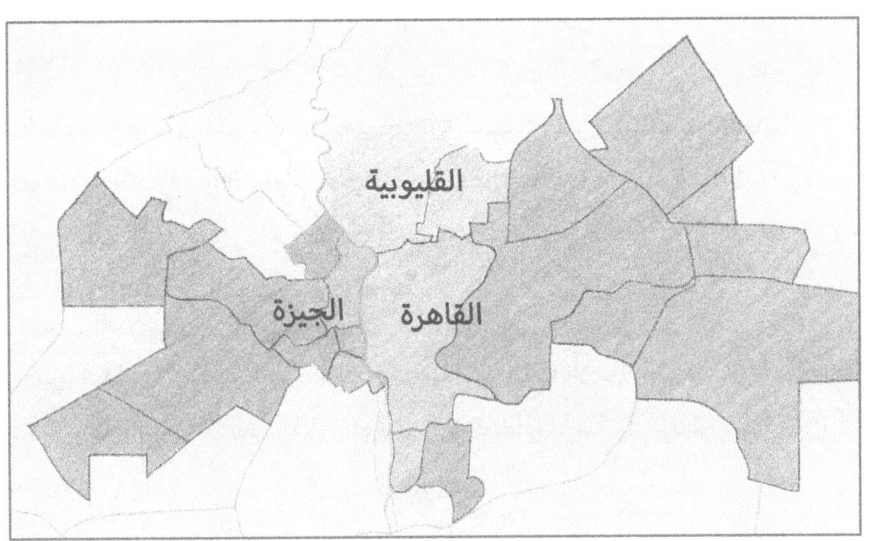

القليوبية

الجيزة   القاهرة

نشأة القاهرة وتطورها

القاهرة مش بس مدينة، دي حكاية مستمرة من ألف سنة وأكثر. من أيام
الفسطاط اللي بناها عمرو بن العاص سنة ٦٤٢م، لحد القاهرة الفاطمية في
القرن العاشر، ولحد القاهرة الحديثة، المدينة دي دايمًا كانت في قلب التاريخ.

الفاطميين أسسوا "القاهرة" كعاصمة جديدة سنة ٩٧٠م، وبنوا الأزهر، اللي بقى
واحد من أقدم الجامعات في العالم. بعدهم جم المماليك والعثمانيين
والملوك المصريين وكل واحد ساب بصمته المعمارية والثقافية.

في القرن التسعتاشر، حاول الخديوي إسماعيل يخلي القاهرة شبه باريس،
وبدأت تظهر شوارع واسعة، ومباني أوروبية، وحدائق عامة. بعد ثورة ١٩٥٢،
المدينة كبرت بسرعة، والامتداد السكاني وصل لمناطق مكانش حد يتخيل إنها
تبقى سكنية.

النهارده، القاهرة بقت مزيج من العصور: فيها آثار إسلامية، عمارات من القرن
العشرين، وأبراج حديثة. تاريخها مش معروض في متحف، لكنه جزء حيّ من
الحياة اليومية للناس.

الجيزة والقليوبية

لما نقول "القاهرة الكبرى"، بنقصد التكتل الحضري اللي بيضم محافظات القاهرة، والجيزة، والقليوبية. الجيزة موجودة غرب النيل، ومعروفة طبعًا بالأهرامات وأبو الهول، لكن هي كمان محافظة سكنية ضخمة، فيها أحياء متنوعة زي الدقي، المهندسين، وفيصل.

الجيزة فيها توازن غريب بين التاريخ والحاضر: جنب الأهرامات فيه قرى لسه بتعتمد على الزراعة، وفي نفس الوقت، فيه تجمعات سكنية حديثة ومولات تجارية.

أما القليوبية فهي الامتداد الشمالي للقاهرة، وفيها مدن صناعية زي شبرا الخيمة، العبور، والخانكة. القليوبية بتمثل البوابة بين القاهرة والدلتا، وبيعيش فيها ملايين من الناس اللي بيشتغلوا في القاهرة أو حواليها.

رغم إن المحافظتين ليهم إدارات مستقلة، لكن حياتهم اليومية مترابطة مع القاهرة لدرجة إن فيه ناس مش بتعرف الفرق بين الحدود الإدارية.

الزحام، العشوائيات، والعمران

أكبر تحدي بيميز القاهرة الكبرى هو الزحام. عدد السكان فيها عدّى الـ٢٠ مليون نسمة، والشوارع دايمًا زحمة، سواء بالعربيات أو بالبشر. النقل العام مش دايمًا كافي، والمواصلات العشوائية بقت واقع يومي.

العشوائيات ظهرت نتيجة لهجرة الريف للمدينة من أول الستينات وما بعدها. ناس كتير بنوا مساكن من غير تخطيط في أطراف المدينة، أو حتى جوه الكتل السكنية. رغم التحديات، إلا إنّ الأماكن دي فيها حياة مجتمعية مترابطة.

الدولة بدأت برامج لتطوير العشوائيات، زي نقل السكان لمناطق زي "الأسمرات" و"بشاير الخير". كمان فيه مشاريع ضخمة زي العاصمة الإدارية

الجديدة، اللي هدفها تخفيف الضغط عن وسط القاهرة.

العمران الحديث بقى جزء من حياة الناس، بس دايمًا فيه قلق من فقدان الهوية المعمارية، وغياب التخطيط بعيد المدى.

القاهرة الثقافية والإدارية

القاهرة مش بس العاصمة السياسية، لكنها كمان العاصمة الثقافية لمصر والعالم العربي. فيها كل المؤسسات الرسمية: رئاسة الجمهورية، البرلمان، الوزارات، والمحاكم الكبرى.

لكن الأهم من ده هو دورها في الثقافة. القاهرة هي مقر الإذاعة والتليفزيون، والصحف، ودور النشر الكبرى. كمان فيها المسارح، ودور السينما، والمراكز الثقافية.

الأوبرا المصرية، وقصر الثقافة، ومركز الإبداع، كلهم بيقدموا فعاليات فنية متنوعة. كمان فيها مكتبات عظيمة زي مكتبة القاهرة الكبرى، ومتاحف زي المتحف المصري في التحرير، والمتحف القومي للحضارة.

وطبعًا ما نقدرش ننسى الأزهر والكنايس القديمة في مصر القديمة، والجامعات الكبرى زي جامعة القاهرة وعين شمس. المدينة بتجمع بين التنوع الديني والثقافي، وبتقدم صورة حية عن هوية مصر المتعددة الثقافات.

رغم الزحام والتحديات، القاهرة لسه عندها روح خاصة، صدى صوتها بيرن في الزقاق، في نِدا البياع المتجول، في الكتب اللي على الرصيف، وفي حكايات الناس اللي عايشة فيها. هي مدينة مش سهلة صحيح، لكن مستحيل تلاقي لها بديل.

Comprehension Questions

1. أيه أول مدينة إسلامية اتبنت في مصر؟ ومين بناها؟

2. ليه الفاطميين أسسوا القاهرة الجديدة سنة ٩٧٠م؟

3. إزاي حاول الخديوي إسماعيل يغير شكل القاهرة في القرن ال ١٩؟

4. أيه اللي حصل للقاهرة بعد ثورة ١٩٥٢ من ناحية النمو السكاني؟

5. أيه اللي بنقصده بمصطلح "القاهرة الكبرى"؟

6. أيه أشهر المعالم اللي موجودة في الجيزة؟

7. ليه القليوبية بتُعتبر بوابة بين القاهرة والدلتا؟

8. أيه أسباب ظهور العشوائيات حوالين القاهرة؟

9. أيه المشروعات اللي بدأت الدولة تعملها لتطوير العشوائيات؟

10. أيه المؤسسات الثقافية والفنية المهمة اللي موجودة في القاهرة؟

Discussion / Essay Prompts

1. هل تفتكر إن القاهرة محتاجة عاصمة إدارية جديدة فعلًا؟ ولا الحل في تطويرها من جوه؟

2. أيه رأيك في إن القاهرة مدينة فيها تاريخ من ألف سنة لحد دلوقتي: هل ده نقطة قوة ولا عبء؟

3. لو جيت تزور القاهرة لأول مرة، أيه الأماكن اللي هتكون أولويتك؟ وليه؟

٦
الدلتا وكنوزها

Where the Nile divides into its northern branches, it creates the Delta—a vast triangle of green fields that has always been central to Egypt's survival. This fertile region provides much of the country's food and is home to  bustling cities like Mansoura, Tanta, and Zagazig, each with its own character and traditions. The Delta is not only about agriculture; it is also a place of trade, crafts, learning, and a distinct cultural identity shaped over centuries. In this unit, you will explore both the well-known landmarks and the hidden treasures that make the Delta a vital part of Egypt's story.

Pre-Reading Questions

١. ليه الدلتا تعتبر منطقة مهمة جدًا في مصر؟

٢. في رأيك، أيه العلاقة بين الزراعة والصناعة في الدلتا؟

٣. هل تعتقد إن الصناعات اليدوية لسه ليها مستقبل في عصر التكنولوجيا؟

Vocabulary

Read the definitions below. Each one matches a bold word or phrase in the text. Try to guess the terms first, then find them in context as you read. Answers are at the back of the book.

1. أدوات من الطين المحروق، منتشرة في القرى

2. أكلة تقليدية معمولة من سمك مملح مشهورة في الدلتا

3. الناس اللي بيزرعوا الأرض وعايشين من شغلها

4. شيخ صوفي مشهور مدفون في طنطا ومقامه مقصد للزوار

5. صناعة تقليدية في بعض قرى الغربية بالاعتماد على النسج اليدوي

6. فقدان مساحات من الأرض الزراعية بسبب العمران أو الماية

7. محافظة زراعية وصناعية عاصمتها الزقازيق

8. محافظة في الدلتا عاصمتها المنصورة، مشهورة بالتعليم والصحة

9. محافظة في الدلتا عاصمتها طنطا، مشهورة بالصناعات والحياة الدينية

10. نشاط صناعي مشهور في دمياط، من أول الورش الصغيرة للمصانع الكبيرة

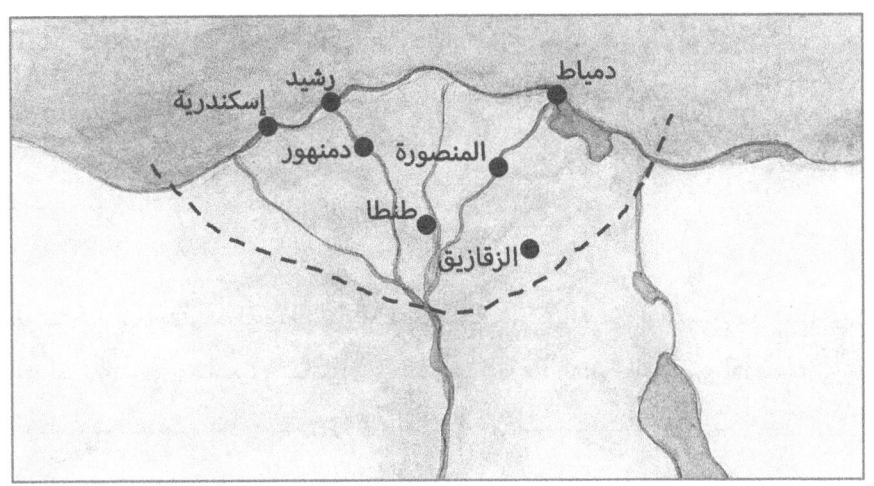

لمحافظات: الدقهلية، الشرقية، الغربية، إلخ

دلتا النيل بتعتبر قلب مصر الزراعي والتاريخي. بتمتد من أول ما النيل بيتفرّع شمال القاهرة لحد ما يوصل البحر المتوسط، الأراضي هناك خصبة، والناس ليهم طباع مميزة.

الدلتا بتضم محافظات كتير، أهمها: الدقهلية، الغربية، الشرقية، كفر الشيخ، البحيرة، المنوفية، ودمياط. كل محافظة ليها طابع خاص، ولهجة محلية، ونشاط اقتصادي بيختلف حسب موقعها.

الدقهلية مثلًا معروفة بالمنصورة، اللي كانت دايمًا مركز للعلم والثقافة، وفيها جامعة كبيرة ومستشفيات متطورة.

الغربية فيها طنطا، اللي تعتبر مدينة دينية وروحية بوجود جامع السيد البدوي، وكمان فيها صناعات تقليدية زي حلاوة المولد والنسيج.

الشرقية محافظة زراعية بامتياز، لكن كمان فيها نشاط تجاري كبير، خصوصًا في الزقازيق.

كل محافظة من دول عندها شبكة كبيرة من القرى، وكل قرية ليها إنتاج معين، من قطن، قمح، خضار، فواكه، أو منتجات ألبان. الدلتا بتعتمد على التكامل بين المحافظات دي، وده اللي بيخليها دايمًا مليانة حركة ونشاط.

الزراعة والصناعة في الدلتا

الدلتا هي سلة غذاء مصر. التربة الطينية الخصبة هناك من أخصب الأراضي في العالم، وبتنتج محاصيل أساسية زي القمح، الرزّ، القطن، الدرة، والطماطم. الزراعة هناك مش بس مصدر رزق، لكنها كمان أسلوب حياة بتتوارثه أجيال ورا أجيال.

الفلاحين في الدلتا عندهم خبرات تقليدية، بيعرفوا يتعاملوا مع فصول السنة، والآفات، ونظم الري. في نفس الوقت، بدأ يظهر اهتمام بتحديث الزراعة باستخدام تكنولوجيا الري بالتنقيط، والبذور المُعدلة.

لكن الزراعة مش كفاية، عشان كده ظهرت صناعات بتعتمد عليها. فيه مصانع تعبئة الفواكه والخضار، مصانع غزل ونسيج بتشتغل على القطن المصري، ومصانع ألبان صغيرة وكبيرة.

كمان فيه نشاط صناعي تقليدي، زي السجاد اليدوي في بعض قرى الغربية، وصناعة الأثاث في دمياط.

في المقابل، بتواجه الدلتا تحديات بيئية خطيرة: زي تآكل الأراضي بسبب الزحف العمراني، وارتفاع منسوب المياه المالحة في بعض المناطق الساحلية. ومن هنا أصبح الحفاظ على التوازن بين التنمية والبيئة هناك مسألة حياة أو موت.

المدن الكبرى: المنصورة، طنطا، الزقازيق

مدن الدلتا مش بس محاور إدارية، لكنها كمان مراكز للحركة الثقافية والتعليمية والاقتصادية.

المنصورة، عاصمة الدقهلية، واحدة من أهم المدن في شمال مصر. اتشهرت بمستشفاها الجامعي، ونشاطها التعليمي، وكمان بأسلوب الحياة النشيط. وسط البلد هناك دايمًا فيه حركة، وكافيهات، ومحلات بتفتح للصبح.

طنطا، قلب الغربية، مدينة ليها طابع روحاني بسبب وجود جامع السيد البدوي، اللي بيجذب آلاف الزوار، خاصة وقت المولد. في نفس الوقت، هي مدينة تجارية نشيطة، وفيها جامعات وأسواق كبيرة.

الزقازيق، عاصمة الشرقية، مدينة سريعة النمو، فيها خليط من الريف والحضر، وبتتميز بوجود أعداد كبيرة من الشباب والطلاب. جامعة الزقازيق ليها دور مهم في الحياة الثقافية والتعليمية للمنطقة.

المدن دي بتعكس وجه جديد للدلتا: شباب بيحاول يلاقي فرص، ستات بتشتغل في التعليم والتمريض، ومحلات حديثة جنب الأسواق التقليدية.

ورغم إن أغلبها بعيد عن الأضواء الإعلامية، لكنها فعليًا بتشكّل نبض مهم في جسد مصر.

كنوز الدلتا المخفية

بعيد عن الزراعة والمدن الكبرى، الدلتا فيها كنوز مش دايمًا ظاهرة للناس. في دمياط، مثلًا، واحدة من أهم صناعات الأثاث في الشرق الأوسط، وبتتميز بورش صغيرة بتشتغل بإيد حرفيين مهرة.

في كفر الشيخ، في بحيرات طبيعية زي بحيرة البرلس، مليانة طيور مهاجرة وصيادين بيرجعوا كل يوم بقوت يومهم.

وفي القرى، لسه فيه ناس بتشتغل في الحرف اليدوية، زي الفخار، والنحاس، والخوص. الصناعات دي ممكن تكون صغيرة، لكنها بتمثل تراث مهم، ونمط حياة بيقاوم النسيان.

حتى الأكل في الدلتا ليه طابع خاص: الفطير، الجبنة القديمة، الفسيخ، وكلها بتعكس علاقة الناس بالأرض والزمن وفصول السنة.

الكنوز دي تستحق اهتمام أكتر، سواء من الحكومة أو المجتمع، علشان ما تضيعش وسط زحمة العصر الحديث.

Comprehension Questions

1. ليه الدلتا بتعتبر قلب مصر الزراعي؟

2. أيه أهم المحافظات اللي بتكوّن منطقة الدلتا؟

3. أيه اللي بيميز مدينة طنطا عن باقي مدن الدلتا؟

4. أيه دور الزقازيق في محافظة الشرقية؟

5. أيه المحاصيل الأساسية اللي بتتزرع في الدلتا؟

6. إزاي الصناعات في الدلتا مرتبطة بالزراعة؟ هات أمثلة.

7. أيه التحديات البيئية اللي بتواجه الدلتا في الوقت الحالي؟

8. أيه أهمية بحيرة البرلس في كفر الشيخ؟

9. أيه الحرف اليدوية اللي لسه موجودة في القرى؟

10. إزاي المأكولات التقليدية في الدلتا بتعكس علاقة الناس بالأرض والزمن؟

Discussion / Essay Prompts

1. هل شايف إن الصناعات اليدوية في الدلتا تستحق دعم أكبر من الدولة؟ ليه؟

2. هل شايف إن المدن الكبرى في الدلتا مظلومة إعلاميًا مقارنةً بالقاهرة واسكندرية؟

3. لو هتزور الدلتا، أيه الأماكن أو الأنشطة اللي تحب تجربها؟

٧

الصعيد: الجنوب اللي فوق

Stretching from Beni Suef down to Aswan, Upper Egypt (known in Arabic as الصعيد) is a region rich in history, tradition, and resilience. Its name comes from its higher elevation above sea level, even though it lies to the south on the map. Villages and towns line the narrow strip of fertile land along the Nile, surrounded by desert on both sides, creating a unique way of life that has endured for centuries. Upper Egypt is also a cultural heartland, where family ties, customs, and a strong sense of identity continue to shape daily life. In this unit, you'll learn about the land, the people, and the spirit that give the region its distinctive character.

Pre-Reading Questions

١. أيه اللي بيميز الصعيد عن باقي مناطق مصر في رأيك؟

٢. هل شايف إن التقاليد بتساعد المجتمع ولا بتقيّد حريته؟

٣. ليه تعتقد إن مدن زي الأقصر وأسوان مشهورة على مستوى العالم؟

Vocabulary

Read the definitions below. Each one matches a bold word or phrase in the text. Try to guess the terms first, then find them in context as you read. Answers are at the back of the book.

1. الجزء الجنوبي من الصعيد الممتد من أسيوط لحد أسوان

2. الجزء الشمالي من الصعيد الأقرب للدلتا والقاهرة

3. الخدمات الأساسية زي المية، الطرق، والكهربا

4. العادات واللغة والثقافة اللي بتميز النوبيين

5. انتقال الناس من الصعيد لمدن تانية جوه مصر علشان الشغل

6. علاقات الدم والعيلة اللي بتحدد مكانة الفرد في المجتمع

7. مدينة صعيدية معروفة بدورها الثقافي والتعليمي

8. مدينة في الصعيد مشهورة بأديرتها التاريخية وجامعتها

9. معبد جنائزي شهير للملكة حتشبسوت في الأقصر

10. منطقة في جنوب أسوان ليها تاريخ وثقافة مميزة

الصعيد الأعلى والصعيد الأدنى

الصعيد، أو "وجه قبلي" زي ما بيتقال عليه رسميًا، بيتقسم لجزئين: الصعيد الأدنى، أو الصعيد الشمالي، اللي بيشمل المحافظات الأقرب للدلتا، زي الفيوم، بني سويف، والمنيا؛ والصعيد الأعلى، المعروف ب "الصعيد الجواني"، وده بيبدأ من أسيوط لحد أسوان.

رغم إن التسميات توحي بالعكس، لكن "الأعلى" معناها الأعلى عن منسوب البحر، بالمقارنة بالصعيد الأدنى. مش من ناحية الاتجاه الجغرافي شمال-جنوب.

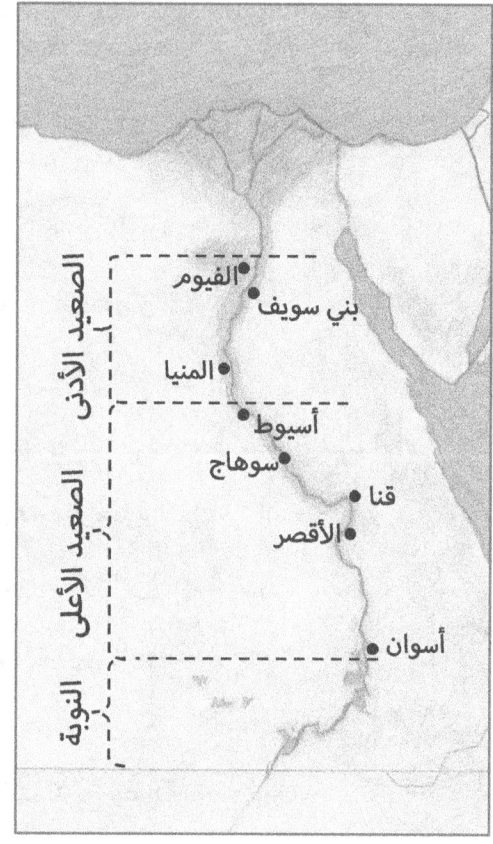

الصعيد الأعلى والأدنى ليهم خصائص جغرافية واقتصادية واجتماعية مميزة. الأرض هناك دايمًا قريبة من النيل، وبعدها الصحرا، وده خلى شكل العمران عبارة عن شريط ضيق على جانبي النهر.

الصعيد الأدنى غالبًا فيه نشاط زراعي أكبر، وارتباط أقرب بالمركز (القاهرة)، بينما الصعيد الأعلى بيتميز بالتماسك الاجتماعي الأقوى، والحفاظ على العادات والتقاليد.

الحياة بين التقاليد والتغيير

الحياة في الصعيد كانت دايمًا بتجمع بين التمسك بالتراث الأصيل والمحاولات التدريجية للتكيّف مع العصر.

بتفضل الروابط القبلية والعائلية ليهم دور مهم جدًا، والقرى هناك بتعيش بروح جماعية واضحة. العلاقات بين الناس مبنية على الاحترام، والنظام الاجتماعي فيه قواعد غير مكتوبة.

لكن التغيرات التكنولوجية، والتعليم، والهجرة الداخلية (للعمل في القاهرة أو المدن الساحلية)، كلها عوامل خلت الصعيد يتغير تدريجيًا.

الستات في الصعيد بقى ليهم دور أكبر في التعليم وسوق العمل، وبدأت مفاهيم جديدة تنتشر وسط الشباب عن الحرية الشخصية، والمشاركة المجتمعية، والمساواة.

رغم كده، لسه فيه تحديات، بالأخص في القرى الصغيرة: زي ضعف البنية التحتية، قلة الخدمات الصحية، ونقص فرص العمل.

وفي نفس الوقت، الناس بقت أكتر وعي، وبتطالب بحقوقها، وبتشتغل على تطوير مجتمعها من جوا.

مدن مهمة: أسيوط، سوهاج، قنا، الأقصر، أسوان

كل مدينة في الصعيد ليها شخصية مستقلة، وتاريخ طويل.

أسيوط مثلًا كانت دايمًا مركز ثقافي وتعليمي، فيها جامعة كبيرة، ونشاط أدبي، وهي من أولى المحافظات اللي خرج منها مفكرين وأدباء كبار.

سوهاج مدينة بتجمع بين الهدوء والروح الدينية، فيها أديرة تاريخية، وجامعة

نشيطة.

قنا معروفة بصناعاتها التقليدية، وبإنها نقطة وصل بين شمال وجنوب الصعيد،
وفيها مجتمع منسجم.

الأقصر مدينة بتعيش على الماضي المجيد. معابدها، زي الكرنك والدير
البحري، بيجذبوا ملايين السياح،
لكنها كمان مدينة حديثة بتحاول
توازن بين السياحة والحياة
اليومية.

معبد الكرنك

أسوان هي بوابة مصر على
أفريقيا. مدينة ساحرة على
ضفاف النيل، وفيها تنوع ثقافي كبير، خصوصًا مع وجود النوبة.

المدن دي مش بس مراكز إدارية، لكنها كمان محاور للتعليم، والتجارة،
والسفر، ولكل واحدة فيها نبض وهوية خاصة بيها.

النوبة والهوية النوبية

النوبة، المنطقة اللي بتقع في جنوب أسوان، ليها تاريخ طويل وثقافة فريدة.
النوبيين ليهم لغتهم الخاصة، وعاداتهم، وموسيقاهم، وزيهم التقليدي،
وحتى عمارتهم اللي بتميز القرى النوبية.

تاريخيًا، النوبة كانت مملكة مستقلة في أوقات كتير، وكان ليها علاقات تجارية
وثقافية مع مصر الفرعونية. بعض الفراعنة كانوا من أصول نوبية، وأثرهم لسه
باين في الآثار والنصوص القديمة.

لكن النوبة واجهت تحديات كبيرة، خصوصًا مع بناء السد العالي في الستينات،
واللي أدى لتهجير كتير من سكانها، وغرق قرى بالكامل تحت بحيرة ناصر.

رغم كده، حافظ النوبيين على هويتهم، وفيه محاولات حالية لإحياء اللغة، والثقافة، ومطالبات بحق العودة لبعض المناطق القديمة.

الهوية النوبية جزء أصيل من التنوع المصري، وهي نموذج لقوة التعدد والاندماج.

النهارده، كتير من النوبيين فنانين، موسيقيين، ومثقفين ليهم تأثير عميق في المشهد الثقافي المصري، وبيقدّموا وجه مختلف وجميل عن الجنوب.

Comprehension Questions

1. ليه تسمية "الأعلى" و"الأدنى" مش مرتبطة بالشمال والجنوب جغرافيًا؟

2. أيه اللي بيخلي العمران في الصعيد ياخد شكل شريط ضيق حوالين النيل؟

3. أيه اللي بيميز النشاط الاقتصادي في الصعيد الأدنى مقارنةً بالصعيد الأعلى؟

4. أيه أهم العوامل اللي بتأثر على الحياة الاجتماعية في القرى الصعيدية؟

5. إزاي اتغير دور الستات في الصعيد في الفترة الأخيرة؟

6. أيه التحديات اللي بتواجه القرى الصغيرة في الصعيد؟

7. ليه أسيوط ليها مكانة ثقافية وتعليمية مميزة؟

8. أيه اللي بيميز الأقصر كمدينة سياحية وتاريخية؟

9. أيه تأثير بناء السد العالي على النوبة وسكانها؟

10. أيه الجهود اللي بيعملها النوبيين علشان يحافظوا على هويتهم؟

Discussion / Essay Prompts

1. هل تعتقد إن الهجرة من الصعيد للمدن الكبرى إيجابية ولا سلبية؟ وليه؟

2. هل التقاليد الصعيدية بتمثل عائق قدام التغيير الاجتماعي ولا عامل استقرار؟

3. في رأيك، أيه اللي ممكن يتعلمه باقي المصريين من النوبيين؟

٨
قناة السويس وسينا

Few places in Egypt carry as much global importance as the Suez Canal. Since its opening in the 19th century, it has stood as both an engineering marvel and a symbol of Egypt's modern history, linking seas, continents, and economies. But just beyond its waters lies Sinai,

a land of rugged mountains, sweeping deserts, and deep cultural roots. Together, the canal and Sinai tell a story of connection and separation, of global trade routes and local traditions, of conflict, resilience, and renewal. This unit explores how these two regions, so different in nature, are both central to Egypt's identity and its place in the world.

Pre-Reading Questions

1. ليه قناة السويس تعتبر من أهم الممرات المائية في العالم؟

2. أيه اللي بيميز مدن القناة عن باقي المدن المصرية؟

3. في رأيك، ليه سينا ليها مكانة خاصة عند المصريين؟

Vocabulary

Read the definitions below. Each one matches a bold word or phrase in the text. Try to guess the terms first, then find them in context as you read. Answers are at the back of the book.

١. إن الدولة تستولي على مشروع أو شركة وتخليه ملك عام

٢. السكان الأصليين في سينا، ليهم تقاليد وأسلوب حياة خاص

٣. تنظيمات غير قانونية بتستخدم العنف وتهدد الأمن

٤. توسعة للقناة افتتحت سنة ٢٠١٥ لتسريع مرور السفن

٥. حرب بين مصر وإسرائيل انتهت بتحرير سينا

٦. مدينة ساحلية في جنوب سينا مشهورة بالشعاب المرجانية والغطس

٧. مدينة مفتوحة للتأثيرات الدولية والتنوع الثقافي زي بورسعيد زمان

٨. مشروعات كبيرة بتعملها الدولة لدمج كل الأقاليم في الاقتصاد الوطني

٩. مناطق تجارية في بورسعيد بتبيع بضايع معفية من الجمارك

١٠. هجوم عسكري سنة ١٩٥٦ شاركت فيه بريطانيا وفرنسا وإسرائيل ضد مصر

قناة السويس وأهميتها

قناة السويس مش مجرد ممر مائي. دي واحدة من أهم الشرايين التجارية في العالم، وبتربط بين البحرين الأبيض والأحمر، وبتختصر وقت وتكلفة نقل البضايع بين آسيا وأوروبا بشكل كبير.

افتُتِحت القناة سنة ١٨٦٩ بعد مشروع ضخم شارك فيه آلاف العمال المصريين. من وقتها، فضلت القناة مصدر قوة اقتصادية واستراتيجية لمصر، وسبب لصراعات دولية ومحلية، زي العدوان الثلاثي سنة ١٩٥٦.

تأميم القناة بقرار من جمال عبد الناصر كان نقطة تحول في التاريخ المصري، وخلّى القناة رمز للسيادة الوطنية.

في ٢٠١٥، افتتحت مصر "قناة السويس الجديدة"، وهو مشروع توسعة لتسريع مرور السفن وزيادة الدخل القومي.

النهارده، القناة بتمر منها آلاف السفن كل سنة، وبتحقق مليارات من العملة الصعبة. لكن أهميتها مش بس اقتصادية؛ دي كمان ورقة سياسية لمصر في علاقاتها مع العالم، ومصدر فخر للناس، كإنها معجزة هندسية من صنع المصريين.

مدن القناة: السويس، الإسماعيلية، بورسعيد

على ضفاف القناة، ظهرت مدن ليها طابع فريد وتاريخ غني: السويس، والإسماعيلية، وبورسعيد.

السويس، عند مدخل القناة من جهة الجنوب، معروفة بتاريخها المقاوم وصمودها في الحروب. شعبها عنده روح وطنية عالية، والمدينة كانت دايمًا بوابة لمصر على البحر الأحمر.

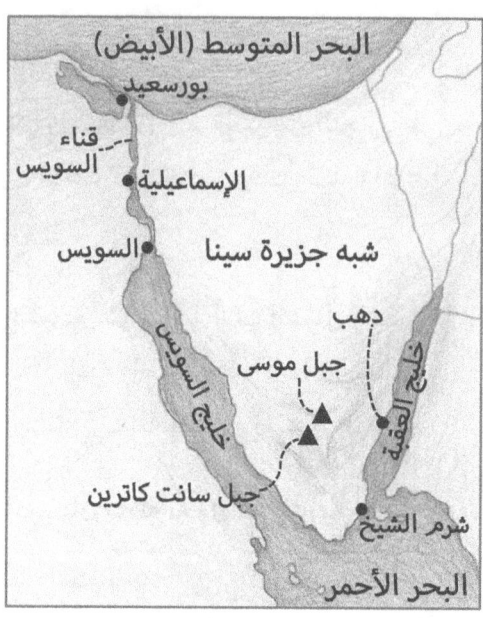

الإسماعيلية، اللي بتعتبر المدينة المركزية للقناة، بتجمع بين الطابع الأوروبي والتقاليد المصرية. اتأسست وقت حفر القناة، وفيها أحياء بتعكس تاريخ طويل من الاستيطان والاختلاط الثقافي. كمان الإسماعيلية بقت مركز إداري مهم، وفيها مقرات هيئة قناة السويس، وبتشهد نشاط اقتصادي كبير.

بورسعيد، على المدخل الشمالي، كانت لفترة طويلة "مدينة عالمية" بمعنى الكلمة. فيها طابع معماري مميز، وأسواق حرة، وثقافة متميزة. لعبت دور بطولي في حروب مصر، وفضلت رمز للمقاومة والفخر الشعبي.

كل مدينة من دول ليها علاقة خاصة بالقناة. سكانها مرتبطين بيها، شغلهم بيعتمد عليها، وحياتهم اليومية متأثرة بحركتها. بالإضافة لكده، المدن دي بتعكس مزيج من الحداثة والتاريخ، من الانفتاح على العالم والتمسك بالهوية المحلية.

سينا: الطبيعة، السكان، الأمن

شبه جزيرة سينا، المنطقة الواسعة اللي بتمتد بين خليجي السويس والعقبة، كانت دايمًا ليها مكانة خاصة في قلب مصر، جغرافيًا وروحيًا.

الطبيعة في سينا ساحرة ومختلفة عن باقي مصر: جبال عالية في الجنوب، زي جبل موسى وجبل سانت كاترين؛ صحرا واسعة في الوسط؛ وشواطئ خلابة على

البحرين. ده غير الشعاب المرجانية في دهب وشرم الشيخ اللي بتجذب آلاف السيّاح سنويًا.

البيئة دي مش بس سياحية، لكن كمان غنية بالمعادن والثروات الطبيعية، وده بيخليها ذات أهمية اقتصادية كبيرة.

السكان الأصليين في سينا، خصوصًا البدو، ليهم ثقافة وعادات مختلفة. عايشين في مجتمعات مترابطة، بيحافظوا على تقاليدهم، وبيعتبروا الصحرا بيتهم. ورغم إن علاقتهم مع الدولة مرت بتقلبات، لكنهم جزء لا يتجزأ من النسيج الوطني.

الجانب الأمني في سينا كان دايمًا حاضر في المشهد. سينا كانت ساحة لمعظم حروب مصر الحديثة، من ١٩٥٦، لـ ١٩٦٧، ولحد حرب أكتوبر ١٩٧٣. وبعد التحرير الكامل، فضلت مسألة التنمية والأمن تحدي كبير.

في السنين الأخيرة، واجهت سينا مشاكل أمنية بسبب وجود جماعات مسلحة. الدولة قامت بحملات عسكرية وأمنية مكثفة لمواجهتهم، وفي نفس الوقت شغالة على مشاريع تنموية كبيرة: طرق، مدارس، مستشفيات، ومزارع.

الهدف هو دمج سينا بالكامل في التنمية القومية، وتثبيت الأمن والاستقرار بشكل دائم.

الناس في مصر عندهم علاقة وجدانية بسينا. مش بس علشان موقعها أو مواردها، لكن كمان علشان رمزيتها في الوجدان المصري كأرض مقدسة وغالية.

دير سانت كاترين وجبل موسى

Comprehension Questions

1. ليه قناة السويس مهمة للتجارة العالمية؟

2. إمتى اتفتحت قناة السويس؟ ومين شارك في حفرها؟

3. ليه قرار عبد الناصر بتأميم القناة كان نقطة تحول في التاريخ المصري؟

4. أيه الهدف من مشروع قناة السويس الجديدة سنة ٢٠١٥؟

5. أيه المدن اللي بتقع على ضفاف القناة؟

6. ليه مدينة بورسعيد كان ليها طابع عالمي؟

7. أيه اللي بيميز الطبيعة في سينا عن باقي مصر؟

8. مين السكان الأصليين في سينا؟ وأيه أسلوب حياتهم؟

9. أيه الحروب اللي حصلت في سينا في القرن العشرين؟

10. أيه التحديات الأمنية اللي بتواجهها سينا في السنين الأخيرة؟

Discussion / Essay Prompts

1. هل شايف إن قناة السويس مجرد مشروع اقتصادي ولا رمز وطني؟ ليه؟

2. في رأيك، أيه التوازن المطلوب بين الأمن والتنمية في سينا؟

3. هل تعتقد إن السياحة في سينا ممكن تكون مفتاح لحل مشاكلها الاقتصادية؟

٩

البحر الأحمر وسياحة الشواطئ

Stretching along Egypt's eastern coast, the Red Sea has become one of the country's brightest gems. Once little more than quiet fishing villages, places like Hurghada, Sharm el-Sheikh, and Marsa Alam now draw visitors from every corner of the globe. Beneath the clear waters lies a world of coral reefs and vibrant marine life, while on land, luxury resorts and bustling promenades have transformed the shoreline into a hub of international tourism. Yet the Red Sea is more than a playground for travelers; it is a delicate environment, a source of livelihood, and a stage where Egypt balances development with preservation.

Pre-Reading Questions

١. تفتكر ليه البحر الأحمر بقى من أشهر المقاصد السياحية في العالم؟

٢. هل شايف إن الغوص نشاط ترفيهي بس ولا له قيمة تعليمية وبيئية؟

٣. في رأيك، أيه التحديات اللي ممكن تهدد مستقبل السياحة في البحر الأحمر؟

Vocabulary

Read the definitions below. Each one matches a bold word or phrase in the text. Try to guess the terms first, then find them in context as you read. Answers are at the back of the book.

1. أنواع مش منتشرة من الأسماك أو الكائنات بتعيش في البحر الأحمر

2. الأثر اللي بتعمله أنشطة الإنسان أو الطبيعة على البيئة حوالينا، زي الهوا، الميّة، الأرض، والنباتات والحيوانات

3. بلد صغيرة أهلها بيعتمدوا على الصيد كمصدر رزق أساسي

4. تسهيلات وفنادق ومطاعم وأنشطة بتتعمل للسيّاح

5. تكوينات بحرية ملونة بتعيش فيها أنواع كتيرة من الكائنات

6. خروج مواد بترولية في البحر بتلوث المايّة وبتضر الكائنات

7. رمي الزبالة، ممكن يأثر على البيئة

8. زيادة المنتجعات والفنادق والأنشطة في منطقة معينة

9. طيور بتسافر بين القارات وبتقف تستريح في المحميات

10. نشاط سياحي ورياضي لاكتشاف أعماق البحر والشعاب المرجانية

الغردقة، شرم الشيخ، مرسى علم

ساحل البحر الأحمر في مصر بيمتد من السويس لحد الحدود مع السودان، وعلى طول الساحل ده فيه مدن سياحية بقت من أشهر الأماكن في الشرق الأوسط والعالم.

الغردقة، عاصمة محافظة البحر الأحمر، كانت في الأصل قرية صيد بسيطة، بس مع الوقت، اتحولت لمدينة عالمية. من التمانينات، بدأت تتبني فيها الفنادق والمنتجعات، وبقت بتستقبل مئات الألوف من السيّاح كل سنة.

شرم الشيخ، في جنوب سينا، بقت جوهرة السياحة المصرية. المدينة مبنية على نظام دقيق، ومنظمة جدًا، وفيها خدمات سياحية على أعلى مستوى. المؤتمرات الدولية، والقمم السياسية، والفعاليات العالمية بقت بتتعمل هناك، وده زوّد شهرتها وأهميتها.

مرسى علم، ناحية الجنوب، اتطورت بشكل أبطأ من غيرها، بس دلوقتي بقت من أسرع المناطق من حيث النمو السياحي. اللي بيميز مرسى علم هو الطبيعة البِكر، والشعاب المرجانية اللي لسه ما تأثرتش كتير بالزحمة.

كل مدينة من دول ليها شخصية مختلفة: الغردقة مدينة مفتوحة ومرنة، شرم الشيخ منظمة وراقية، ومرسى علم هادية وطبيعية. السيّاح اللي بيجوا بيختاروا حسب التجربة اللي بيدوروا عليها، وفي كل الأحوال، بيلاقوا بحر جميل، شمس ساطعة، وخدمة ممتازة.

الغوص، المحميات، وجمال الشعاب المرجانية

البحر الأحمر معروف بمايته الصافية، وده بيخلي تجربة الغوص هناك من الأفضل في العالم. الشعاب المرجانية في مصر متنوعة، وغنية بالألوان، وفيها كائنات بحرية نادرة.

أماكن زي راس محمد، محمية أبو جالوم، جزيرة الجفتون، والشعاب القريبة من مرسى علم، بقت مواقع مشهورة جدًا للغواصين. فيه ناس بتيجي مخصوص من آخر الدنيا علشان تنزل غطسة في الأماكن دي.

الغوص مش بس نشاط سياحي، لكنه كمان بيخلي الناس تشوف عالم تاني تحت الميّة. في بعض الشعاب، ممكن تشوف أسراب من الدلافين، سلاحف بحرية، وحتى أنواع من أسماك القرش، وكل ده في بيئة طبيعية ساحرة.

فيه كمان محميات طبيعية حوالين البحر الأحمر، فيها حياة برّية نادرة، زي الغزلان، التعالب، وبعض أنواع الطيور المهاجرة. المحميات دي مش بس للعرض، لكن كمان لحماية النظام البيئي.

المرشدين والغواصين المحترفين بيشتغلوا على توعية السيّاح بعدم لمس المرجان، وعدم رمي مخلفات في البحر، علشان نحافظ على البيئة دي.

التوسع السياحي والتحديات البيئية

مع النجاح الكبير للسياحة في البحر الأحمر، حصل توسّع عمراني وسياحي كبير. فنادق، منتجعات، مطارات، طرق، وكهربا... مشاريع ضخمة اتنفذت علشان تدعم قطاع السياحة.

بس مع التوسع، بدأت تظهر مشاكل بيئية خطيرة. الشعاب المرجانية، اللي بتاخد مئات السنين علشان تتكون، ممكن تتدمر في لحظات بسبب هلب اترمى غلط غلط أو تسريب زيت من مركب.

كمان البنا العشوائي، أو التخلص من المخلفات بشكل غير منظم، بيأثر على جودة الميّة والحياة البحرية. ده غير التوسعات اللي بتقرب من المحميات وبتضغط على الكائنات اللي عايشة هناك.

علشان كده، ظهرت مبادرات للحفاظ على البيئة:

- منظمات أهلية بدأت تشتغل مع الدولة علشان تفرض قواعد للغوص ورحلات التنزه.
- ابتدت حملات تنضيف للشواطئ وقاع البحر.
- تدريب العاملين في السياحة على ممارسات صديقة للبيئة.
- تشجيع السياحة المستدامة، يعني سياحة بتراعي البيئة وما تضرهاش.

الدولة كمان بدأت تحط قوانين لتقنين التوسعات العمرانية ومتابعة تأثيرها البيئي، خصوصًا في الأماكن الحساسة. فيه محاولات لتحقيق التوازن بين الاستفادة الاقتصادية من السياحة، والحفاظ على الموارد الطبيعية.

نجاح السياحة في البحر الأحمر مش بس مرهون بالخدمات أو جمال الطبيعة، لكنه كمان مرتبط بقدرتنا على الحفاظ على المكان، علشان يفضل جميل وآمن للأجيال الجاية.

Comprehension Questions

1. إزاي السياحة اتطورت في البحر الأحمر من التمانينات لحد النهارده؟

2. ليه السيّاح بييجوا مخصوص علشان الغوص في البحر الأحمر؟

3. أيه اللي بيميز الشعاب المرجانية في مصر؟

4. أيه الكائنات البحرية اللي ممكن يشوفها الغواصين هناك؟

5. إزاي المرشدين والغواصين بيحافظوا على البيئة البحرية؟

6. أيه نوعية المشروعات اللي اتبنت لدعم السياحة في البحر الأحمر؟

7. أيه المخاطر اللي بتهدد الشعاب المرجانية؟

8. إزاي البنا العشوائي بيأثر على البحر والحياة البحرية؟

9. أيه المبادرات اللي اتعملت للحفاظ على البيئة الساحلية؟

10. ليه مهم ندرب العاملين في السياحة على ممارسات صديقة للبيئة؟

Discussion / Essay Prompts

1. في رأيك، هل ممكن السياحة تكون مستدامة فعلًا في البحر الأحمر؟

2. أيه الحلول اللي تقترحها علشان نحافظ على الشعاب المرجانية من التدمير؟

3. لو كنت سائح في البحر الأحمر، أيه التصرفات اللي هتعملها علشان تحافظ على البيئة؟

۱۰
واحات وعجايب

Far from the crowded cities and fertile Nile Valley, Egypt's deserts hold unexpected worlds of green. The oases (Siwa, Dakhla, Kharga, Farafra, and others) have for centuries been places of refuge, trade, and unique culture. Each oasis

has its own story: ancient temples, traditional architecture, hidden springs, and star-filled skies that seem endless. They are spaces where life has adapted to the harshest conditions, creating communities deeply tied to land and water. In this unit, we explore the landscapes, traditions, and natural marvels that make Egypt's oases so distinctive.

Pre-Reading Questions

1. ليه الواحات مهمة في بلد صحراوي زي مصر؟

2. في رأيك، هل الحياة البسيطة في الواحات أحسن ولا أصعب من الحياة في المدن؟

3. هل تعتقد إن السياحة البيئية ممكن تبقى مصدر رزق مهم لأهل الواحات؟

Vocabulary

Read the definitions below. Each one matches a bold word or phrase in the text. Try to guess the terms first, then find them in context as you read. Answers are at the back of the book.

1. أشكال طبيعية نتجت عن الرياح أو العوامل البيئية

2. تراب مبلول بالميّة، بيتحوّل لمادة لزجة، ويُستخدم في الفخار والبناء

3. تراث موسيقي بيتوارثه الناس في الأفراح والمناسبات

4. خليط من الطين والملح بيتبني بيه بيوت تقليدية في سيوة

5. عادة استقبال الزوار بالترحيب والأكل والشاي

6. علاقات قوية بين أهالي الواحات مبنية على التعاون والترابط

7. فترة جمع المحاصيل الزراعية من الأرض

8. فراغات طبيعية في الجبال، أحيانًا بتكون فيها نقوش أو رسومات قديمة

9. قنوات جوفية بتنقل الماية من الآبار للمزارع من غير هدر

10. مناطق من الرمل الناعم مش ثابتة تحت الرجلين

واحات مشهورة: سيوة، الداخلة، الخارجة، الفرافرة

في وسط الصحرا، بعيد عن الزحمة والمدن الكبيرة، فيه عالم تاني اسمه الواحات. واحات مصر مش بس مصدر ميّة في قلب الجفاف، لكنها كمان أماكن ليها طابع خاص، وتاريخ طويل، وطبيعة ساحرة.

من أشهر الواحات: سيوة، الداخلة، الخارجة، والفرافرة، وكل واحدة منهم ليها طابعها وشخصيتها المميزة.

سيوة، مثلًا، موجودة في أقصى غرب مصر، قريّبة من الحدود الليبية. الواحة دي مشهورة بثقافتها الخاصة، وسكانها اللي بيتكلموا أمازيغي بجانب العربي.

فيها معابد قديمة زي معبد آمون، وفيها بحيرات مالحة، وعين كليوباترا، وبيوت مبنية من مادة اسمها الكرشيف [مزيج من الطين والملح]. سيوة كمان مشهورة بزيت الزتون والتمور.

معبد آمون في سيوة

الداخلة والخارجة في الوادي الجديد، وبيعتبّروا من أخصب الواحات. فيهم أراضي زراعية واسعة، وقرى فيها بيوت طينية ورسومات جميلة على الحيطان. الخارجة كمان فيها آثار رومانية ومتاحف، وبتعتبر العاصمة الإدارية للوادي الجديد.

الفرافرة، الأصغر والأهدى، قريبة من الصحرا البيضا، وبتتميز بالهدوء والسكينة. عدد سكانها قليّل، لكن طبيعتها فريدة، خصوصًا بالليل، لما السما بتتزين بالنجوم بشكل مبهر.

الحياة التقليدية في الواحات

الحياة في الواحات ليها إيقاع مختلف. الناس هناك عايشين ببساطة، ومرتبطين بالطبيعة والمية. الزراعة هي الأساس، خصوصًا زراعة النخيل، الزتون، الحبوب، والخضروات.

الناس هناك بيستخدموا تقنيات ريّ تقليدية، زي القنوات الجوفية أو "الفقارات"، اللي بتوصل المية من الآبار للمزارع بأقل هدر ممكن.

العمارة في الواحات بسيطة لكن عملية. البيوت بتتبني من الطين، علشان تعزل الحرارة في الصيف، وتحافظ على الدفا في الشتا. البيوت دي كمان ليها لمسة جمالية فريدة، بتميزها رسومات وزخارف مستوحاه من تراث الواحة.

الضيافة جزء مهم جدًا من حياة الناس هناك. الزائر دايمًا مرحب بيه، وأول حاجة تتقدم له هي التمر والشاي. المجتمعات هناك متماسكة، والعلاقات قوية بين الجيران والعائلات.

رغم إن التكنولوجيا بدأت تدخل الواحات، لكن لسه فيه حرص على الحفاظ على التراث والعادات. فيه حفلات، أغاني شعبية، ورقصات تقليدية بيتوارثها جيل بعد جيل، خصوصًا في المناسبات الكبيرة زي الأفراح أو موسم الحصاد.

الظواهر الجيولوجية: الجبال، الكهوف، الرمال المتحركة

من الحاجات اللي بتميز واحات مصر إنها مش بس مناطق خضرا، لكن كمان محاطة بطبيعة جيولوجية مبهرة.

الصحرا البيضا، مثلًا، جنب الفرافرة، تعتبر واحدة من أغرب الأماكن في العالم.

الأرض كلها هناك متغطية بصخور جيرية لونها أبيض، والأشكال الناتجة عن الرياح عاملة تكوينات غريبة شبه الفطر، أو الحيوانات. المنظر هناك بالليل تحت ضوء القمر بيبقى ساحر.

فيه كمان الكهوف اللي موجودة في مناطق زي جبل الداخلة أو جبل الكريستال. الكهوف دي أحيانًا بيكون فيها نقوش أو رسومات بدائية، وبتحكي عن حياة الإنسان القديم في الصحرا. وناس كتير من الجيولوجيين بيجوا يدرسوها علشان يعرفوا معلومات أكتر عن تطور الأرض.

الرمال المتحركة كمان موجودة في بعض المناطق حوالين الواحات، ودي مناطق رمل ناعم جدًا بيكون مش ثابت تحت تحت الرجلين. صحيح مش بالخطورة اللي بنشوفها في الأفلام، لكنها ممكن تكون فخ لو الشخص مش واخد باله أو ماشي من غير دليل.

الجبال حوالين الواحات كمان ليها دور في تشكيل الجو والمناخ، وبتكون دايمًا خلفية مدهشة للواحات، سواء في الشروق أو الغروب.

Comprehension Questions

1. أيه اللي بيميز واحات مصر عن باقي الصحرا؟

2. ليه سيوة مشهورة بثقافتها المميزة؟

3. أيه المواد اللي بيستخدمها أهل الواحات في بناء البيوت؟ وليه؟

4. أيه المحاصيل الأساسية اللي بتتزرع في الواحات؟

5. إزاي بيتم نقل الماية للزراعة في الواحات؟

6. أيه دور الضيافة في حياة الناس في الواحات؟

7. أيه الحفلات أو العادات اللي لسه متوارثة في الواحات؟

8. أيه اللي ممكن يلاقيه الباحثين أو الجيولوجيين في الكهوف حوالين الواحات؟

9. هل الرمال المتحركة خطيرة زي ما بنشوفها في الأفلام؟ ليه أو ليه لأ؟

10. إزاي الجبال حوالين الواحات بتأثر على المنظر والمناخ؟

Discussion / Essay Prompts

1. هل تحب تعيش فترة في واحة زي سيوة أو الداخلة؟ ليه أو ليه لأ؟

2. في رأيك، هل التمسك بالتراث في الواحات بيساعد ولا بيعيق التنمية؟

3. إزاي ممكن مصر تستفيد من الظواهر الطبيعية الفريدة في جذب السيّاح؟

١١
محافظات مصر الرسمية

Modern Egypt is organized into 27 governorates, each with its own character, challenges, and role in the nation's life. Some are vast deserts with only small populations, while others are bustling urban centers where millions live side by side. This system of administrative divisions has roots stretching back to pharaonic times, yet it continues to evolve with the country's political and economic needs. In this unit, we look at how the governorates are structured, how they are managed, and how life differs between Egypt's urban, rural, and border regions.

Pre-Reading Questions

1. ليه تقسيم مصر لمحافظات مهم في رأيك؟

2. هل تعتقد إن الخدمات الحكومية متوزعة بعدل بين كل المحافظات؟

3. في رأيك، أيه الفرق بين الحياة في محافظة حضرية ومحافظة ريفية؟

Vocabulary

Read the definitions below. Each one matches a bold word or phrase in the text. Try to guess the terms first, then find them in context as you read. Answers are at the back of the book.

١. أدوات بصرية بتوضح توزيع السكان والخدمات والمشاريع

٢. المسؤول الأول عن إدارة شؤون المحافظة بقرار من الدولة

٣. انتقال الناس من الريف للمدن بحثًا عن شغل أو تعليم

٤. برنامج حكومي لتطوير القرى وتحسين الخدمات والبنية التحتية

٥. سيطرة الحكومة من العاصمة على باقي المناطق

٦. طريقة انتشار الناس في البلد بين المدن والريف

٧. محافظات على أطراف مصر ليها اعتبارات أمنية وتنموية خاصة

٨. محافظة يغلب عليها الطابع الزراعي والحياة الأهدى

٩. محافظة يغلب عليها الطابع المدني والكثافة السكانية العالية

١٠. هيئات منتخبة من الناس لمتابعة الخدمات واتخاذ قرارات محلية

عدد المحافظات وأسمائها

مصر متقسّمة إداريًا لـ ٢٧ محافظة، وكل محافظة ليها حدود واضحة، ومُحافِظ متعين بيدير شؤونها. التقسيم ده مش جديد؛ من أيام الفراعنة، كانت مصر متقسمة لأقاليم، وفضلت فكرة التقسيم موجودة على مر العصور، مع تغييرات حسب الظروف السياسية والاقتصادية.

الـ٢٧ محافظة هما: القاهرة، الجيزة، القليوبية، إسكندرية، البحيرة، كفر الشيخ، الغربية، المنوفية، الدقهلية، الشرقية، دمياط، بورسعيد، الإسماعيلية، السويس، شمال سينا، جنوب سينا، بني سويف، الفيوم، المنيا، أسيوط، سوهاج، قنا، الأقصر، أسوان، البحر الأحمر، الوادي الجديد، ومطروح.

فيه محافظات ضخمة من حيث المساحة زي الوادي الجديد، اللي بتمثل أكتر من ٤٠٪ من مساحة مصر، لكن سكانها قليلين جدًا، وفيه محافظات صغيرة زي بورسعيد أو دمياط، بس عدد السكان فيهم أكبر بكتير.

إزّاي بتدار المحافظات؟

كل محافظة بيكون على رأسها محافظ، بيتم تعيينه بقرار من رئيس الجمهورية. المحافظ بيشرف على تنفيذ السياسات الحكومية في مجالات زي التعليم، الصحة، النقل، الإسكان، وغيرها. كمان بيراقب المحليات، وبياخد قرارات تخص الحياة اليومية في محافظته.

بجانب المحافظ، فيه المجالس المحلية، ودي المفروض تكون منتخبة من الشعب. دورها هو الرقابة على الخدمات، ومناقشة الميزانيات، والمشاركة في اتخاذ القرارات المحلية. لكن الحقيقة إن دور المجالس دي في بعض الأحيان بيكون محدود، وبيحتاج دعم أقوى من كده علشان يحقق التوازن بين السلطة المركزية والسلطة المحلية.

المحافظات بتشتغل مع الوزارات المركزية، وده بيخلي فيه تنسيق مستمر بين القاهرة وباقي الأقاليم. بس أحيانًا بيكون فيه بطء في تنفيذ المشاريع، أو تداخل في المسؤوليات، وده بيتسبب في بعض المشاكل على أرض الواقع.

الفروق بين المحافظات الحضرية والريفية

مش كل المحافظات ليها نفس الطبيعة. فيه محافظات حضرية زي القاهرة، إسكندرية، وبورسعيد، وفيه محافظات ريفيّة أو مختلطة زي المنوفية، الفيوم، وسوهاج.

المحافظات الحضرية بيكون فيها كثافة سكانية عالية، بنية تحتية أكبر، وخدمات متنوعة أكثر. الناس هناك متعودين على الحياة السريعة، وبيتعاملوا مع التكنولوجيا بشكل يومي.

أما المحافظات الريفية، فالحياة فيها أهدى، وغالبًا الاقتصاد بيعتمد على الزراعة، أو الصناعات الصغيرة. التعليم والخدمات الصحية ممكن تكون أقل في الكفاءة أو الانتشار، وده بيخلق فجوة بين الريف والحضر.

فيه كمان محافظات حدودية زي شمال سينا أو مطروح، ودي ليها طبيعة خاصة، لأن فيها اعتبارات أمنية، وقبائل، وتحديات تنموية مختلفة.

ومن ضمن المشاكل اللي بتواجه المحافظات الريفية كمان هو الهجرة الداخلية، لأن ناس كتير بتسيب القرى وتروح المدن تدور على شغل أو تعليم أحسن.

توزيع السكان والخدمات

توزيع السكان في مصر مش متوازن أبدًا. حوالي ٩٥٪ من المصريين عايشين على شريط ضيق حوالين نهر النيل والدلتا، والباقي متوزعين على المدن الساحلية، أو في واحات ومناطق صحراوية محدودة.

المناطق زي القاهرة والجيزة بتمثل ضغط ضخم على الخدمات بسبب النمو السكاني، في حين إن أماكن تانية فيها مساحات فاضية لكنها ناقصها خدمات أساسية.

توزيع الخدمات الحكومية مش دايمًا بيكون عادل. أحيانا المدارس والمستشفيات ومراكز الشباب بتكون متكدسة في بعض المحافظات، ونادرة في محافظات تانية. الحكومة بتحاول مؤخرًا توصل الخدمات دي للمناطق المحرومة من خلال مبادرات زي "حياة كريمة"، اللي بتركز على تطوير القرى والبنية التحتية.

كمان بيتم استخدام تقنيات جديدة علشان ترصد الاحتياجات بدقة، زي الخرايط الجغرافية، وتحليل البيانات السكانية، علشان توزيع الخدمات يبقى مبني على أرقام مش مجرد تقديرات.

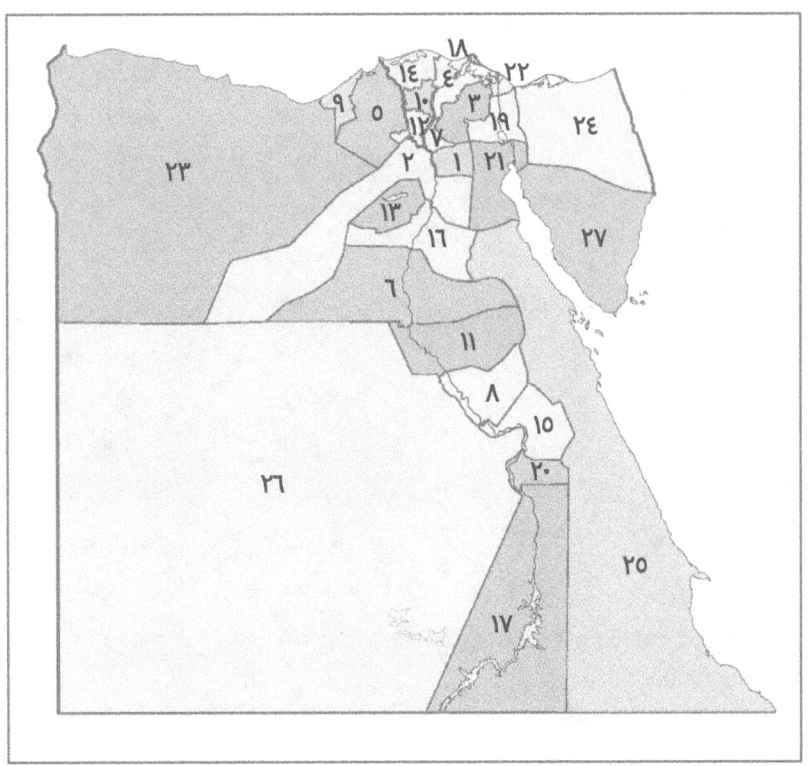

المساحة (كم^2)	عدد السُّكّان	العاصمة	المحافظة	
٣,٠٨٥	١٠,٣٣٨,٥٠٨	القاهرة	القاهرة	١
٨٥,١٥٣	٩,٦٣٤,٠٦٣	الجيزة	الجيزة	٢
٤,٩١١	٨,٠٠٧,٩٣٤	الزقازيق	الشرقية	٣
٣,٥٣٨	٧,١١٧,٩٠٠	المنصورة	الدقهلية	٤
٩,٨٢٦	٦,٩٧٠,٨٦٦	دمنهور	البحيرة	٥
٣٢,٢٧٩	٦,٤٥٢,٨٠٧	المنيا	المنيا	٦
١,١٢٤	٦,٢٠٦,٣٠٨	بنها	القليوبية	٧
١١,٠٢٢	٥,٨٣٤,٣١٤	سوهاج	سوهاج	٨
٢,٢٩٩	٥,٠٩٣,٠٧٩	إسكندرية	إسكندرية	٩
١,٩٤٢	٥,٤٩٢,٩١٢	طنطا	الغربية	١٠
٢٥,٩٢٦	٥,١٥٨,٠١٥	أسيوط	أسيوط	١١
٢,٤٩٩	٤,٧٩٣,٦٤٠	شبين الكوم	المنوفية	١٢
٦,٠٦٨	٤,١٤٧,٣٦٠	الفيوم	الفيوم	١٣
٣,٤٦٦	٣,٧٦١,٥١٨	كفر الشيخ	كفر الشيخ	١٤
١٠,٧٩٨	٣,٧٠٤,٤٨٣	قنا	قنا	١٥
١٠,٩٥٤	٣,٦٥٣,٠٢٩	بني سويف	بني سويف	١٦
٦٢,٧٢٦	١,٧٨١,١٣٠	أسوان	أسوان	١٧
٩١٠	١,٦٣٢,٤٦٨	دمياط	دمياط	١٨
٥,٠٦٦	١,٤٧٢,٩٠٧	الإسماعيلية	الإسماعيلية	١٩
٢,٤٠٩	١,٤٢٣,٢٧٩	الأقصر	الأقصر	٢٠
٩,٠٠٢	٨٠٠,٦٩١	السويس	السويس	٢١
١,٣٤٤	٧٩٥,٩١٢	بورسعيد	بورسعيد	٢٢
١٦٦,٠٦٤	٥٧٦,٢٨٠	مرسى مطروح	مطروح	٢٣
٢٨,٩٩٢	٥١٦,٢٦٤	العريش	شمال سيناء	٢٤
١١٩,٠٩٩	٤٠٩,٩٦٨	الغردقة	البحر الأحمر	٢٥
٤٤٠,٠٩٨	٢٧٠,٨٣٥	الخارجة	الوادي الجديد	٢٦
٣١,٢٧٢	١١٨,٦٥٩	الطور	جنوب سيناء	٢٧

Source: Wikipedia

Comprehension Questions

1. كام محافظة في مصر دلوقتي؟

2. أيه الدور المفروض تقوم بيه المجالس المحلية؟

3. أيه الفرق بين السلطة المركزية والسلطة المحلية؟

4. أيه المحافظات اللي تعتبر حضرية؟ وأيه اللي يميزها؟

5. أيه اللي بيميز المحافظات الريفية عن الحضرية؟

6. ليه المحافظات الحدودية ليها طبيعة خاصة؟

7. أيه سبب الهجرة الداخلية من الريف للمدن؟

8. إزاي توزيع السكان في مصر غير متوازن؟

9. أيه الهدف من مبادرة "حياة كريمة"؟

10. إزاي استخدام الخرايط الجغرافية بيساعد في توزيع الخدمات؟

Discussion / Essay Prompts

1. هل تعتقد إن لازم يكون للمجالس المحلية سلطة أكبر؟ ليه أو ليه لأ؟

2. في رأيك، أيه التحديات اللي بتواجه المحافظات الريفية أكتر من الحضرية؟

3. هل شايف إن إعادة توزيع السكان ممكن تحل مشاكل الزحمة في القاهرة والجيزة؟

١٢
المناطق الثقافية وغير الرسمية

Beyond the official map of Egypt's 27 governorates lies another way people describe the country. Egyptians often refer to broad regions like Upper and Lower Egypt, or to more local areas tied to history, dialect, and tradition. These divisions often say  more about identity and belonging than any line drawn on a government map. In this unit, we explore how Egyptians talk about their regions, what these distinctions mean, and how cultural geography shapes daily life.

Pre-Reading Questions

١. في رأيك، ليه الناس بيفضّلوا يستخدموا مسميات زي "وجه بحري" و"قبلي" بدل المحافظات؟

٢. أيه اللي بيخلي اللهجات جزء من الهوية المحلية؟

٣. هل الاختلافات الثقافية بتفرّق المصريين ولا بتغني هويتهم الوطنية؟

Vocabulary

Read the definitions below. Each one matches a bold word or phrase in the text. Try to guess the terms first, then find them in context as you read. Answers are at the back of the book.

1. إحساس الناس بانتماء خاص لمنطقة معينة

2. إحساس بالارتباط والانتماء لبلدك، بيتعبّر عنه بالفخر، وتحمل المسؤولية، وإنك تحس إنك جزء من أرضها وناسها

3. الخصائص اللي بتميز مجتمع من حيث العادات والأسلوب

4. المنطقة الجنوبية الممتدة من الجيزة لحد أسوان

5. المنطقة الشمالية القريبة من البحر المتوسط

6. تمسّك قوي بالتقاليد القديمة في الحياة اليومية

7. تنوع في النطق والكلمات بين منطقة والتانية

8. طريقة الناس في وصف وتحديد المناطق على أساس العادات واللهجة والتاريخ

9. مرونة وتقبّل للتنوع والاختلاف في المجتمعات

10. منطقة بين فرعين النيل: دمياط ورشيد. وليها طابع ولهجة مميزة

الفرق بين التقسيم الرسمي والشعبي

مصر رسميًا متقسّمة لـ ٢٧ محافظة، وكل محافظة فيها مراكز ومدن وقرى. التقسيم ده إداري، الدولة بتستخدمه علشان تدير الخدمات، التعليم، الصحة، والأمن. لكن في نفس الوقت، الناس عندهم تقسيم تاني غير رسمي، بيستخدموه في كلامهم وحياتهم اليومية، وبيعبّر عن تصورهم لهوية الأماكن.

الناس ما بيقولوش "محافظة الدقهلية" دايمًا، لكن بيقولوا "من بلاد الدلتا"، أو "أنا من وجه بحري". وفي الجنوب، تلاقي الناس تقول "أنا من الصعيد" أو "من قبلي"، من غير ما يحددوا المحافظة.

التقسيم الشعبي بيعتمد على عوامل زي التاريخ، اللهجة، العادات، نوع الزراعة، وحتى شكل الأرض. فممكن تلاقي منطقتين في نفس المحافظة، بس أهلهم بيشوفوا نفسهم مختلفين جدًا من ناحية الثقافة والانتماء.

الفرق ده مش بس في المسميات، لكنه كمان بيدل على مدى تعقيد الهوية المصرية، وإنها مش مجرد حدود مرسومة على الخريطة. أحيانا بيكون التقسيم الشعبي إنعكاس أقرب لعلاقة الناس بالبيئة المحيطة. وده ليه دور مهم في تشكيل العلاقات الاجتماعية والانتماء.

وجه بحري ووجه قبلي ووسط الدلتا

من زمان، مصر بتنقسم لوجهين: وجه بحري في الشمال، ووجه قبلي في الجنوب. الكلمة "بحري" معناها قريب من البحر، و"قبلي" معناها في اتجاه القبلة، أو الجنوب.

وجه بحري بيشمل المحافظات القريبة من البحر المتوسط، زي إسكندرية، البحيرة، المنوفية، وغيرها. المناطق دي فيها أراضي زراعية خصبة، عدد سكان كبير، ومدن فيها نشاط صناعي وتجاري كبير.

وجه قبلي بيبدأ من الجيزة وينزل لحد أسوان، وبيضم محافظات زي بني سويف، المنيا، سوهاج، قنا، والأقصر. المناطق دي أقرب للريف التقليدي، وفيها طابع محافظ أكتر، وزراعة بتعتمد على القصب، والنخيل، والزراعة النيلية.

الفرق بين الوجهين مش بس جغرافي، لكنه كمان ثقافي. في وجه بحري، الناس غالبًا لهجتهم أخف، وسلوكهم اجتماعي منفتح شوية. في قبلي، اللهجة بيظهر فيها الطابع العربي القديم بشكل أوضح، وفيها التزام أقوى بالعادات والتقاليد.

"وسط الدلتا" مصطلح بيتقال على مناطق زي الغربية، والمنوفية، والدقهلية، وهي المناطق اللي بين فرعين النيل: دمياط ورشيد.

الاختلاف بين المناطق دي مش بس لغوي، لكنه بيعكس شعور الناس بانتماء خاص للمكان، سواء بسبب شكل الحياة، نوع الزراعة، أو حتى نوع العلاقات الاجتماعية.

رغم ده، فيه تقارب كبير بين الناس في المناسبات والأزمات، والهوية الوطنية بتجمعهم، حتى لو طريقة التعبير مختلفة.

هل فيه اختلاف في اللهجة، العادات، والهوية؟

أيوه، فيه اختلافات واضحة، بس مش بالشكل اللي الناس متخيلاه. في اللهجة مثلًا، اللهجة الصعيديّة مختلفة بشكل ملحوظ عن لهجات الوجه البحري والقاهرة. الاختلافات بتظهر في النطق والمفردات، وده بيديها طابع مميز يعبّر عن الهويّة المحليّة. ورغم كده، اللهجات دي مفهومة في معظمها لباقي المصريين، خصوصًا إن كتير من الصعايدة بيكيّفوا كلامهم لما يتعاملوا مع ناس من برّه الصعيد.

في العادات، تلاقي الصعايدة ملتزمين بالعادات بشكل أقوى: اللبس، الأكل، علاقات الجيرة، والاحتفال بالمناسبات. في وجه بحري، فيه مرونة أكتر، خصوصًا في المدن الكبرى.

أما الهوية، فكتير من الناس في قبلي بيحسوا إنهم ليهم خصوصية، وإن عندهم تاريخ طويل من النضال والعراقة. في وجه بحري، الناس أحيانًا بتتكلم عن الانفتاح والتنوع، خصوصًا في مناطق المواني والمراكز التجارية.

لكن رغم الاختلافات دي، فيه خيط جامع بين كل المصريين: الانتماء للوطن، ومحبة النيل، والتاريخ المشترك. ودي حاجة بتميز مصر، إنها موحدة رغم تنوعها.

Comprehension Questions

1. أيه الفرق بين التقسيم الرسمي والتقسيم الشعبي في مصر؟

2. ليه الناس أحيانًا بيقولوا "من وجه بحري" أو "من قبلي" بدل اسم المحافظة؟

3. أيه العوامل اللي بتحدد التقسيم الشعبي زي ما اتقال في النص؟

4. إزاي التقسيم الشعبي بيعكس علاقة الناس بالبيئة؟

5. أيه اللي بيميز وجه بحري من حيث الأرض والسكان؟

6. أيه اللي بيميز وجه قبلي من حيث الطابع الثقافي والزراعة؟

7. أيه أمثلة على التقاليد اللي لسه محافظة عليها مجتمعات الصعيد؟

8. ليه الناس في وجه بحري بيتكلموا عن الانفتاح والتنوع أكتر؟

9. إزاي بتظهر فكرة الهوية المحلية في كلام الناس عن نفسهم؟

10. رغم كل الاختلافات، أيه الخيط الجامع بين المصريين كلهم؟

Discussion / Essay Prompts

1. في رأيك، اللهجات المصرية المختلفة هل تعتبر ثروة لغوية ولا عقبة في التواصل؟

2. إزاي ممكن الإعلام أو التعليم يستفيدوا من التنوع الثقافي بين المناطق؟

3. هل الوحدة الوطنية في مصر قوية كفاية علشان تتجاوز أي اختلافات محلية؟

Vocabulary Answer Key

Unit 1

6. السد العالي		1. شريان الحياة	
7. موقع استراتيجي		2. الحدود السياسية	
8. قناة السويس		3. وادي النيل	
9. الصعيد		4. الحدود الطبيعية	
10. محافظة		5. مناخ	

Unit 2

6. ملوحة التربة		1. النقل النهري	
7. مشروع قومي		2. الزحف العمراني	
8. دلتا النيل		3. الطمي	
9. أسمدة صناعية		4. بحيرة ناصر	
10. الري بالرش		5. مشروعات سدود	

Unit 3

6. الواحات		1. نمط حياة	
7. بحر الرمال الأعظم		2. الجبل الكريستالي	
8. محمية طبيعية		3. العبابدة والبشارية	
9. معبد آمون		4. المياه الجوفية	
10. السياحة البيئية		5. التنمية المستدامة	

Unit 4

6. مهنة تقليدية	1. مواسم الصيد
7. مرسى علم	2. التنمية العمرانية
8. الموانئ السياحية	3. التجارة البحرية
9. التلوث البحري	4. الشعب المرجانية
10. الغوص	5. المناخ المعتدل

Unit 5

6. شبرا الخيمة	1. الفسطاط
7. العاصمة الإدارية الجديدة	2. القاهرة الفاطمية
8. جامعة القاهرة	3. الزحام
9. العشوائيات	4. الخديوي إسماعيل
10. الأسمرات	5. الأوبرا المصرية

Unit 6

6. تآكل الأراضي	1. الفخار
7. الشرقية	2. الفسيخ
8. الدقهلية	3. الفلاحين
9. الغربية	4. السيد البدوي
10. صناعة الأثاث	5. السجاد اليدوي

Unit 7

٦. الروابط القبلية	١. الصعيد الأعلى
٧. أسيوط	٢. الصعيد الأدنى
٨. سوهاج	٣. البنية التحتية
٩. الدير البحري	٤. الهوية النوبية
١٠. النوبة	٥. الهجرة الداخلية

Unit 8

٦. دهب	١. التأميم
٧. مدينة عالمية	٢. البدو
٨. التنمية القومية	٣. الجماعات المسلحة
٩. الأسواق الحرة	٤. قناة السويس الجديدة
١٠. العدوان الثلاثي	٥. حرب أكتوبر ١٩٧٣

Unit 9

٦. تسريب زيت	١. كائنات بحرية نادرة
٧. التخلص من المخلفات	٢. التأثير البيئي
٨. التوسع السياحي	٣. قرية صيد
٩. طيور مهاجرة	٤. خدمات سياحية
١٠. غوص	٥. شعاب مرجانية

Unit 10

6. مجتمع متماسك	1. تكوينات جيولوجية
7. موسم الحصاد	2. طين
8. كهوف	3. أغاني شعبية
9. الفقارات	4. الكرشيف
10. الرمال المتحركة	5. الضيافة

Unit 11

6. توزيع السكان	1. خرايط جغرافية
7. محافظات حدودية	2. محافظ
8. محافظة ريفية	3. هجرة داخلية
9. محافظة حضرية	4. مبادرة "حياة كريمة"
10. مجالس محلية	5. سلطة مركزية

Unit 12

6. الالتزام بالعادات	1. هوية محلية
7. اختلاف في اللهجة	2. الانتماء للوطن
8. تقسيم شعبي	3. طابع
9. انفتاح	4. وجه قبلي
10. وسط الدلتا	5. وجه بحري

Translations

Unit 1: An Overview of Egypt

Egypt's Geographical Location

Egypt occupies a strategic location that brings together three continents: Africa, Asia, and Europe. It lies in the northeast of Africa and extends along the southeastern coast of the Mediterranean. It also has long coastlines on the Red Sea, giving it a major maritime and commercial advantage.

Another feature that distinguishes Egypt is its control over one of the most important maritime passages in the world: the Suez Canal, which connects the Mediterranean with the Red Sea and facilitates trade between Europe and Asia.

This location has always placed Egypt at the center of events, whether political or economic. Since the days of the pharaohs, Egypt has been a gateway between north and south, east and west. Its position has continued to influence its history, culture, and the challenges it faces. In addition to its outward importance, Egypt's geography and location have also played a major role in shaping its internal divisions, both official and popular.

Natural, Political, and Administrative Borders

Egypt's borders combine natural and political factors. To the north, the Mediterranean separates it from Europe, forming a natural boundary that influences the climate and economy of coastal cities. To the east, the Red Sea and the Sinai Peninsula act as a natural barrier, linking Egypt to Asia through the Isthmus of Suez.

To the south, the border with Sudan is primarily political, drawn across the desert without connection to clear natural features. The same is true to the west, where Egypt's border with Libya runs as a long straight line through the Western Desert.

Natural boundaries, such as coastlines or rugged terrain, helped determine the locations of settlements and ports, while political borders were the result of treaties and historical developments, having changed multiple times over the centuries.

On the administrative level, Egypt is officially divided into 27 governorates, each with an administrative capital and a governor who oversees its affairs. The governorates are further divided into districts, cities, and villages. They vary in size and population, with heavily populated urban governorates such as Cairo and Alexandria, and more rural or desert governorates such as Gharbia and Matruh.

Alongside these official divisions, there are also informal ones widely used by the people, such as Lower Egypt and Upper Egypt, or regions like Sa'id (Upper Egypt) and the Delta. These divisions are rooted in history, geography, and traditions, and they strongly shape local identity.

Climate and Terrain

In addition to its location and borders, Egypt has a predominantly arid desert climate, which means most of the year is sunny with very little rainfall. Yet there are clear differences between north and south. Coastal cities such as Alexandria and Rosetta experience milder winters and more moderate temperatures, particularly because of the influence of the Mediterranean.

In the south, temperatures are higher and the climate is drier. In places like Aswan and Luxor, summer temperatures can exceed forty degrees Celsius.

Egypt's terrain is diverse: the Nile Valley, a narrow strip of fertile land along the river, where the majority of Egyptians live; the Eastern Desert, between the Nile and the Red Sea; and the Western Desert, which covers a vast area of Egypt's territory. In South Sinai, there are high mountains such as Mount Moses (Mount Sinai), while along the Red Sea coast stretches a chain of mountains. This geographical diversity affects economic activity, population distribution, and even local lifestyles.

The Nile: Lifeline of Egypt

The Nile River has been Egypt's lifeblood for thousands of years. Without it, the country would be nothing but vast desert. The Nile begins its journey deep in Africa, passes through several countries, and finally reaches northern Egypt, where it flows into the Mediterranean.

About 95% of Egypt's population lives along its banks, either in the Valley or the Delta, which begins after Cairo. The Delta is an especially fertile agricultural area, producing crops such as wheat, rice, and cotton.

The Nile is not only a source of water and farming, but also a means of transport and fishing, as well as a central part of Egyptian culture and identity. Since the pharaonic era, the river has been the axis of life: temples built on its banks, goods transported by boat, festivals held to mark the flood season.

The Nile also determines the shape of Egypt's economic and social life. The construction of the High Dam at Aswan was a major turning point in the twentieth century. It regulated the flow of water, reduced the danger of floods, and generated hydroelectric power that transformed development in Upper Egypt and the Delta. At the same time, the dam caused environmental and social changes, such as the relocation of some villages and the decline of soil fertility due to the retention of silt. Despite these challenges, the dam remains a cornerstone of

Egypt's water management and a symbol of a national project that reshaped the river and the lives of millions.

Even today, the Nile continues to be Egypt's foundation. Any problem with its sources or Egypt's share of its waters affects the whole country, which is why it remains a central issue in Egypt's water policy and foreign relations.

Unit 2: The Nile and Society

The Delta and the Valley

From the moment you enter Egypt, you notice that most people live along a narrow strip surrounding the Nile River. This area is called "the Valley," one of the most fertile regions in Egypt. The Valley stretches from Aswan in the south up to Cairo. From there, the Nile branches northward into a large triangular shape known as the Nile Delta, divided between the Damietta and Rosetta branches.

The Valley and the Delta are the beating heart of Egypt. Even though they make up less than 5% of Egypt's total land area, over 90% of the population lives there. The reason is simple: fertile soil, nearby water, and favorable conditions for farming.

The Delta is primarily an agricultural zone, with countless villages and relatively developed irrigation and drainage networks. But it also faces major challenges: urban sprawl eating up farmland, pollution, and soil salinity in some coastal areas due to its closeness to the sea.

The Valley, on the other hand, contains major cities like Luxor, Aswan, Qena, and Minya. In the past, villages in the Valley depended entirely on the Nile for drinking water, farming, and fishing. Today, with urban expansion and climate change, there is enormous pressure on water resources.

Agriculture and Transport on the Nile

The Nile is not just a river; it is a lifeline that sustains agriculture, transport, and daily life. Since ancient times, Egyptians have relied on it to cultivate staple crops like wheat, rice, corn, and cotton. The land along the river has always been fertile thanks to the silt deposited by the annual flood—before the construction of the High Dam.

Traditional irrigation depended on waterwheels and canals, but now modern systems such as sprinkler and drip irrigation are increasingly used—an important shift in light of water shortages. The state is also working to improve agricultural methods to save water and maintain production.

As for transport, the Nile has always been an efficient and safe way to move people and goods. Even today, riverboats still operate between cities, especially in the south, and there are also cruise ships carrying tourists between Luxor and Aswan.

However, river transport has declined compared to the past due to the growth of roads, bridges, and rail networks. Still, there are efforts to revive Nile transport to reduce congestion on roads and cut pollution.

Farmers and fishermen depend directly on the Nile, but every household in Egypt is affected indirectly—through food, prices, and water availability. That's why any threat to the Nile, whether domestic or external, impacts the whole society.

The High Dam and Its Impact

In the 1960s, Egypt embarked on a massive project: building the High Dam in Aswan. The goals were clear: control the Nile flood, store water, and generate electricity. This project completely transformed Egyptians' relationship with the river.

Before the dam, the Nile flooded the land every year, renewing the soil's fertility but also causing problems when floods were severe. After the dam was built, water could be fully controlled, allowing the state to regulate irrigation year-round.

The High Dam also provides electricity to a large part of Egypt and was a major step in industrial development. It created Lake Nasser, which stretches hundreds of kilometers and stores vast quantities of water.

But despite its benefits, there have also been negative consequences. The absence of the silt carried by the flood led to a loss of soil fertility, forcing farmers to rely more heavily on chemical fertilizers. Some fish species declined, and the ecosystem was affected.

Controlling the Nile placed greater responsibility on the state for water management. With population growth, the challenges have increased. In recent decades, Egypt has also faced water crises due to dam projects in upstream countries, especially in Ethiopia.

Even so, the High Dam remains a symbol of a successful national project and one of the greatest achievements in modern Egyptian history. It combines national pride with the ongoing challenges that require constant solutions.

Unit 3: The Desert Is Not Just Sand

The Western Desert

The Western Desert covers about two-thirds of Egypt's land area and separates the Nile Valley from the Libyan border. Although the word "desert" makes us imagine barren land, in reality it holds remarkable geological and geographical diversity. There are mountain ranges, massive sand dunes, and green oases set against golden-yellow sand.

Its most famous feature is the Great Sand Sea, which includes some of the largest dunes in the world, attracting adventurers and campers. There are also rocky areas with rare geological formations, such as the Crystal Mountain and the White Desert, which is covered with bright white limestone rocks that look as if they belong to another world.

The Western Desert was also the stage for important historical events, especially during World War II, when battles between Allied and Axis forces took place in the area of El Alamein.

Today, the state is working to make use of this vast desert area through agricultural and residential projects and by increasing reliance on solar energy. With the expansion of infrastructure, new roads have begun to connect the desert to the Delta and the Valley, making travel and investment easier.

The Eastern Desert

The Eastern Desert is less well-known than the Western Desert but no less important. It stretches between the Nile Valley and the Red Sea, covering about 22% of Egypt's land. Its terrain is more rugged than the Western Desert, with high mountains separating it from the coast, such as Mount El Shayeb and Mount Galala.

This desert is extremely rich in minerals. Since the time of the pharaohs, it has been a source of gold, copper, and limestone, and to this day it contains active mines and new exploration zones. It also serves as a gateway to ports on the Red Sea, such as Safaga and Quseir, which are vital hubs for international trade.

It is home to nature reserves such as Wadi El Gemal, which shelters a wide variety of wildlife including plants, gazelles, and rare birds. The region is also inhabited by Bedouin tribes like the Ababda and the Bishari, who still maintain their traditions and way of life despite modernization.

The state is developing the Eastern Desert through the creation of industrial zones, the expansion of road networks, and connecting coastal cities to Upper Egypt—strengthening its economic and strategic role.

Egypt's Oases

Amid Egypt's vast desert expanses, the oases appear like green jewels breaking the monotony of the sand. The most famous are Siwa, Bahariya, Dakhla, Kharga, and Farafra. Each has its own character, unique history, and local community with distinct traditions.

Siwa, for example, is known for its Amazigh heritage, its distinctive language, its sulfur springs, and its natural beauty. It contains historical landmarks such as the Temple of Amun and the "Mountain of the Dead."

The oases are not only agricultural areas but also cultural centers with traditional houses, markets, schools, and health clinics. Residents grow palm trees, olives, and vegetables, relying on groundwater from springs and wells.

In recent years, the oases have become important destinations for eco-tourism and medical tourism, thanks to their pure air, natural springs, and the calm they offer far from crowded cities. They also hold great investment potential in sustainable agriculture and solar energy.

At the same time, they face challenges such as water scarcity, climate change, and migration to larger cities, which affects population stability and the local economy.

Life in the Desert

Life in the desert is not easy, but it is not impossible either. Bedouin communities have lived there for centuries and learned to adapt to harsh conditions. They rely on mobility, raising camels and goats, and making wise use of natural resources.

Today, desert life is beginning to change. New villages are being built, roads are reaching further, and services are being extended to people who were long isolated. Schools and medical centers now exist even in remote areas.

Still, problems remain: isolation, limited job opportunities, and scarce resources. With climate change, some areas have become more vulnerable to drought. At the same time, many desert residents migrate to cities in search of better opportunities, which threatens the survival of ancient local cultures.

Despite this, Egypt's deserts hold enormous potential for sustainable development—in eco-tourism, renewable energy, and modern agriculture. With careful planning, they could shift from marginalized zones to vital hubs for Egypt's future.

Life in the desert teaches patience, self-reliance, and the value of simplicity— qualities that can be deeply meaningful in today's fast-paced, technology-driven world.

Unit 4: The Seas and the Coasts

The Mediterranean Coast

Egypt's northern coast overlooks the Mediterranean Sea and stretches from the border at Rafah in the east to Sallum in the west, a distance of about 1,000 kilometers. This region has always held great strategic and historical importance. Cities such as Alexandria, Port Said, and Damietta are not only ports but also significant cultural and commercial centers.

Alexandria in particular has a special place; from the time of the Greeks until today, it has always been a city bridging East and West. It is home to one of Egypt's largest ports and is also renowned for its university and world-famous library.

The moderate climate and relative humidity make the northern coast suitable for agriculture, especially olives and figs. In addition, it has become one of the most popular tourist destinations, particularly in the summer, when thousands of Egyptians head to the coastal cities and tourist villages.

In recent years, however, growing urban development along the coast has sparked debate about its impact on the coastal environment and the balance between investment and preserving nature.

The Red Sea Coast

Egypt's eastern coast overlooks the Red Sea and extends from Suez in the north to Halayeb and Shalateen in the south. This area is less densely populated than the northern coast but has become one of the most important tourist regions in Egypt and worldwide.

Cities such as Hurghada, Marsa Alam, and Ain Sokhna are now globally recognized for their beautiful beaches, rare coral reefs, and crystal-clear waters. The Red Sea is one of the richest seas in terms of biodiversity, attracting divers and tourists from everywhere.

There are also important ports such as Safaga and Suez, which serve trade with the Gulf and Asia. And the coast's proximity to the Suez Canal makes it a vital element in Egypt's economy.

Large projects in solar and wind energy are also being developed in this region, taking advantage of natural resources and supporting the shift toward renewable energy.

Despite its beauty and potential, the coast faces challenges, such as the environmental impact of tourism and the struggle to protect coral reefs in the face of climate change.

Fishing, Trade, and Maritime Tourism

The two seas—the Mediterranean and the Red—are not just water boundaries for Egypt, but sources of life and economic opportunity. Fishing, for example, is a traditional profession in many coastal communities, especially in Rosetta, Damietta, Suez, and Safaga.

Fishermen's lives depend on fishing seasons, types of fish, and the weather. In some areas, traditional techniques are still in use, while in others, modern fishing with advanced equipment has appeared.

Maritime trade is a cornerstone of the economy. The Suez Canal, for example, connects the two seas and generates major revenue for Egypt through transit fees. There are also major ports such as Alexandria, Port Said, and Suez, which receive ships from around the world and play a crucial role in exports and imports.

Maritime tourism has become a promising sector. It is not only about diving and beaches but also about cruises and tourist marinas that host yachts and cruise ships.

There is growing interest in developing coastal infrastructure: docks, resorts, and corniches. At the same time, environmental awareness is essential to protect the seas and prevent marine pollution, which can affect marine life and human health.

The two seas have always been a source of inspiration for Egyptians, from fishermen's tales to folk songs, from Pharaonic heritage to modern reality. Today, their future depends on smart planning that balances development with environmental preservation.

Unit 5: Greater Cairo

The Origins and Development of Cairo

Cairo is not just a city; it is a continuous story of over a thousand years. From Fustat, built by Amr ibn al-As in 642 CE, to Fatimid Cairo in the tenth century, to today's modern metropolis, the city has always been at the heart of history.

The Fatimids founded "Cairo" as a new capital in 970 CE and built al-Azhar, which became one of the oldest universities in the world. After them came the Mamluks, the Ottomans, and the Egyptian kings, each leaving their own architectural and cultural imprint.

In the nineteenth century, Khedive Ismail tried to make Cairo resemble Paris, and wide boulevards, European-style buildings, and public gardens began to appear. After the 1952 Revolution, the city expanded rapidly, with the population extending into areas that no one would have imagined as residential neighborhoods.

Today, Cairo has become a blend of eras: Islamic monuments, twentieth-century buildings, and modern towers. Its history is not displayed in a museum; it is a living part of people's daily lives.

Giza and Qalyubia

When we say "Greater Cairo," we mean the urban conglomeration that includes the governorates of Cairo, Giza, and Qalyubia. Giza lies west of the Nile and is, of course, famous for the pyramids and the Sphinx. But it is also a huge residential governorate, with diverse neighborhoods such as Dokki, Mohandessin, and Faisal.

Giza shows a strange balance between history and the present: right next to the pyramids are villages still dependent on agriculture, while nearby stand modern housing complexes and shopping malls.

Qalyubia, on the other hand, is Cairo's northern extension, home to industrial cities such as Shubra al-Kheima, Obour, and Khanka. Qalyubia serves as the gateway between Cairo and the Delta, and millions of people who live there work in Cairo or its surroundings.

Although the two governorates have independent administrations, their daily lives are so intertwined with Cairo that many people do not even know where the administrative boundaries lie.

Congestion, Informal Housing, and Urban Growth

The biggest challenge facing Greater Cairo is congestion. Its population has exceeded 20 million, and the streets are always crowded—whether with cars or with people. Public transportation is not always sufficient, and informal modes of transport have become part of daily life.

Informal housing (slums) appeared as a result of migration from rural areas to the city beginning in the 1960s and beyond. Many people built homes without planning on the outskirts of the city, or even within existing neighborhoods. Despite the challenges, these areas have strong and interconnected community life.

The state has begun programs to redevelop informal housing, such as relocating residents to new neighborhoods like al-Asmarat and Bashayer al-Kheir. There are also major projects like the New Administrative Capital, designed to reduce pressure on central Cairo.

Modern urbanization has become part of people's lives, but there is always concern about losing architectural identity and the absence of long-term planning.

Cultural and Administrative Cairo

Cairo is not only Egypt's political capital but also its cultural capital, and indeed that of the Arab world. It houses all the official institutions: the presidency, parliament, ministries, and major courts.

But more important is its cultural role. Cairo is home to radio and television, newspapers, and major publishing houses. It also has theaters, cinemas, and cultural centers.

The Cairo Opera House, the Cultural Palace, and the Creativity Center all host a variety of artistic events. There are also great libraries such as the Greater Cairo Library, and museums such as the Egyptian Museum in Tahrir Square and the National Museum of Egyptian Civilization.

And, of course, we cannot forget al-Azhar, the old churches of Coptic Cairo, and the major universities like Cairo University and Ain Shams. The city brings together religious and cultural diversity and presents a vivid picture of Egypt's multicultural identity.

Despite the congestion and challenges, Cairo still has its own special spirit. Its echoes ring in the alleyways, in the calls of street vendors, in the books laid out on the sidewalks, and in the stories of the people who live there. It is not an easy city, true, but it is impossible to find an alternative to it.

Unit 6: The Delta and Its Treasures

Governorates: Dakahlia, Sharqia, Gharbia, etc.

The Nile Delta is considered the agricultural and historical heart of Egypt. It stretches from where the Nile branches north of Cairo all the way to the Mediterranean Sea. The land there is fertile, and the people have their own distinctive character.

The Delta includes many governorates, the most important of which are Dakahlia, Gharbia, Sharqia, Kafr El-Sheikh, Beheira, Monufia, and Damietta. Each governorate has its own unique character, local dialect, and economic activity that varies according to its location.

Dakahlia, for example, is known for Mansoura, which has always been a center of learning and culture, with a large university and advanced hospitals.

Gharbia is home to Tanta, a city with religious and spiritual importance thanks to the mosque of al-Sayyid al-Badawi, and it is also known for traditional industries such as ḥalāwat al-moulid (festival sweets) and textiles.

Sharqia is primarily agricultural, but it also has a significant commercial sector, especially in Zagazig.

Each governorate has a wide network of villages, and every village has its own production—cotton, wheat, vegetables, fruits, or dairy products. The Delta relies on the integration of these governorates, which makes it constantly full of movement and activity.

Agriculture and Industry in the Delta

The Delta is Egypt's breadbasket. Its clay soil is among the most fertile in the world, producing staple crops such as wheat, rice, cotton, corn, and tomatoes. Agriculture there is not just a source of livelihood but a way of life passed down through generations.

Farmers in the Delta have deep traditional knowledge, knowing how to deal with the seasons, pests, and irrigation systems. At the same time, there has been growing interest in modernizing agriculture, with the use of drip irrigation technologies and improved seeds.

But agriculture alone is not enough. That is why industries that rely on it have developed: factories for packing fruits and vegetables, spinning and weaving factories that work with Egyptian cotton, and both large and small dairy factories.

There are also traditional industries such as handwoven carpets in some villages of Gharbia and furniture making in Damietta.

On the other hand, the Delta faces serious environmental challenges: land loss due to urban sprawl, and rising levels of salty water in some coastal areas. This makes balancing development and the environment a matter of survival.

Major Cities: Mansoura, Tanta, Zagazig

Delta cities are not just administrative centers but also hubs of cultural, educational, and economic activity.

Mansoura, the capital of Dakahlia, is one of the most important cities in northern Egypt. It is famous for its university hospital, its educational role, and its energetic lifestyle. The downtown area is always lively, with cafés and shops open until late at night.

Tanta, the heart of Gharbia, has a spiritual atmosphere due to the presence of the mosque of al-Sayyid al-Badawi, which attracts thousands of visitors, especially during the moulid festival. At the same time, it is a busy commercial city, home to universities and large markets.

Zagazig, the capital of Sharqia, is a rapidly growing city with a mix of rural and urban features. It stands out for its large population of young people and students, with Zagazig University playing a central role in the region's cultural and educational life.

These cities reflect the new face of the Delta: young people searching for opportunities, women working in education and nursing, and modern shops standing alongside traditional markets.

Even if they don't often appear in the media spotlight, they represent a vital pulse within Egypt's body.

The Delta's Hidden Treasures

Beyond agriculture and the major cities, the Delta has treasures that are not always visible to outsiders.

In Damietta, for example, one of the most important furniture industries in the Middle East thrives, built on small workshops run by skilled craftsmen.

In Kafr El-Sheikh, there are natural lakes such as Lake Burullus, home to migratory birds and local fishermen who return every day with their catch.

In villages, people still work in traditional crafts like pottery, copperwork, and weaving with palm fronds. These industries may be small, but they represent important heritage and a way of life that resists being forgotten.

Even the food in the Delta has its own distinctive character: layered pastry (fatīr), aged cheese, feseekh (fermented fish), all of which reflect the people's relationship with the land, time, and the changing seasons.

These treasures deserve greater attention, whether from the government or society, so they are not lost amid the rush of modern life.

Unit 7: Upper Egypt: The South that is Up

Upper and Lower Upper Egypt

Upper Egypt, or Wagh Qibli as it is officially called, is divided into two parts: Lower, or Northern, Upper Egypt, which includes the governorates closest to the Delta, such as Fayoum, Beni Suef, and Minya; and Upper, or Southern, Upper Egypt, known as "El-Sa'eed el-Gawany," which stretches from Asyut down to Aswan.

Although the names may seem confusing, "Upper" here refers to elevation above sea level compared to Lower Upper Egypt—not to the geographical direction of north and south.

Both Upper and Lower Upper Egypt have distinctive geographical, economic, and social features. The land is always close to the Nile, with desert stretching out beyond it, which has made settlements take the form of a narrow strip along both sides of the river.

Lower Upper Egypt generally has more agricultural activity and a closer connection to the center (Cairo), while Upper Upper Egypt is characterized by stronger social cohesion and greater adherence to customs and traditions.

Life Between Tradition and Change

Life in Upper Egypt has always balanced a strong attachment to deep-rooted traditions with gradual attempts to adapt to modern times.

Tribal and family ties continue to play a very important role, and villages live with a strong sense of community. Relationships between people are built on respect, and the social order is maintained by unwritten rules.

But technological changes, education, and internal migration (to Cairo or coastal cities for work) have all contributed to a gradual transformation of Upper Egypt.

Women now have a greater role in education and the labor market, and new ideas have begun to spread among young people regarding personal freedom, community participation, and equality.

Still, challenges remain, especially in smaller villages: weak infrastructure, limited health services, and a lack of job opportunities.

At the same time, however, people have become more aware, demanding their rights and working to improve their communities from within.

Important Cities: Asyut, Sohag, Qena, Luxor, Aswan

Each city in Upper Egypt has its own character and long history.

Asyut, for example, has always been a cultural and educational hub, with a large university and active literary life. It was among the first governorates to produce major thinkers and writers.

Sohag is a city that combines tranquility with a strong religious spirit, with historic monasteries and an active university.

Qena is known for its traditional industries and as a connecting point between the north and south of Upper Egypt, with a harmonious community.

Luxor lives on its glorious past. Its temples, like Karnak and Deir al-Bahari, attract millions of tourists, but it is also a modern city striving to balance tourism with everyday life.

Aswan is Egypt's gateway to Africa. A beautiful city on the Nile, it has great cultural diversity, especially with the presence of Nubia.

These cities are not only administrative centers but also hubs for education, trade, and travel, each with its own unique pulse and identity.

Nubia and Nubian Identity

Nubia, the region south of Aswan, has a long history and a unique culture. Nubians have their own language, customs, music, traditional clothing, and distinctive architecture that characterizes Nubian villages.

Historically, Nubia was an independent kingdom at various times and maintained commercial and cultural ties with Pharaonic Egypt. Some pharaohs were of Nubian origin, and their influence is still visible in ancient monuments and inscriptions.

But Nubia faced major challenges, especially with the construction of the High Dam in the 1960s, which led to the displacement of many of its people and the flooding of entire villages under Lake Nasser.

Despite this, Nubians preserved their identity, and there are ongoing efforts to revive their language and culture, along with calls for the right to return to some of their ancestral lands.

Nubian identity is an essential part of Egypt's diversity, and it represents a model of the strength of plurality and integration.

Today, many Nubians are artists, musicians, and intellectuals who have a profound influence on Egypt's cultural scene, presenting a different and beautiful face of the south.

Unit 8: The Suez Canal and Sinai

The Suez Canal and Its Importance

The Suez Canal is not just a waterway. It is one of the most important commercial arteries in the world, linking the Mediterranean and the Red Sea and greatly reducing the time and cost of transporting goods between Asia and Europe.

The canal was inaugurated in 1869 after a massive project that involved thousands of Egyptian workers. Since then, it has remained a source of economic and strategic strength for Egypt, and also a reason for both international and domestic conflicts, such as the Tripartite Aggression in 1956.

The nationalization of the canal by Gamal Abdel Nasser was a turning point in Egyptian history, making the canal a symbol of national sovereignty.

In 2015, Egypt inaugurated the "New Suez Canal," an expansion project to speed up ship passage and increase national income.

Today, thousands of ships pass through the canal every year, generating billions in hard currency. But its importance is not only economic; it is also a political card for Egypt in its relations with the world, and a source of pride for Egyptians, as if it were an engineering miracle made by their own hands.

Canal Cities: Suez, Ismailia, Port Said

On the banks of the canal, unique cities with rich histories developed: Suez, Ismailia, and Port Said.

Suez, at the southern entrance to the canal, is known for its history of resistance and steadfastness during wars. Its people have a strong patriotic spirit, and the city has always been Egypt's gateway to the Red Sea.

Ismailia, considered the central city of the canal, combines European character with Egyptian traditions. It was founded during the canal's construction, and its neighborhoods reflect a long history of settlement and cultural interaction. Ismailia also became an important administrative center, housing the headquarters of the Suez Canal Authority and hosting significant economic activity.

Port Said, at the northern entrance, was for a long time a truly "international city." It is distinguished by its unique architecture, free markets, and distinctive culture. It played a heroic role in Egypt's wars and remained a symbol of resistance and popular pride.

Each of these cities has a special relationship with the canal. Their residents are closely tied to it, their jobs depend on it, and their daily lives are affected by its activity. In addition, these cities reflect a mixture of modernity and history, of openness to the world and attachment to local identity.

Sinai: Nature, People, and Security

The Sinai Peninsula, the vast region stretching between the gulfs of Suez and Aqaba, has always held a special place in Egypt's heart, both geographically and spiritually.

Sinai's nature is captivating and unlike the rest of Egypt: high mountains in the south, such as Mount Moses (Mount Sinai) and Mount Saint Catherine; wide deserts in the center; and stunning beaches along both seas. In addition, the coral reefs in Dahab and Sharm El-Sheikh attract thousands of tourists every year.

This environment is not only valuable for tourism but is also rich in minerals and natural resources, giving it great economic importance.

The native inhabitants of Sinai, especially the Bedouins, have their own distinct culture and traditions. They live in tightly knit communities, maintain their customs, and consider the desert their home. Although their relationship with the state has gone through ups and downs, they remain an integral part of the national fabric.

The security dimension has always been present in Sinai. It was the battleground of most of Egypt's modern wars: from 1956, to 1967, and up to the October War of 1973. Even after full liberation, the challenges of development and security remained significant.

In recent years, Sinai has faced security problems due to the presence of armed groups. The state has launched extensive military and security campaigns to confront them, while at the same time carrying out major development projects: roads, schools, hospitals, and farms.

The goal is to fully integrate Sinai into national development and to establish lasting security and stability.

Egyptians have an emotional bond with Sinai—not only because of its location or resources, but also because of its symbolic value in the Egyptian consciousness as a sacred and precious land.

Unit 9: The Red Sea and Beach Tourism

Hurghada, Sharm El-Sheikh, Marsa Alam

Egypt's Red Sea coast stretches from Suez down to the Sudanese border, and along this coastline are tourist cities that have become some of the most famous destinations in the Middle East and the world.

Hurghada, the capital of Red Sea Governorate, was originally a small fishing village, but over time it grew into a global city. Since the 1980s, hotels and resorts began to be built there, and it now receives hundreds of thousands of tourists every year.

Sharm El-Sheikh, in South Sinai, became the jewel of Egyptian tourism. The city is carefully planned and highly organized, offering top-quality tourist services. International conferences, political summits, and global events have been held there, boosting its fame and importance.

Marsa Alam, further south, developed more slowly than the others, but today it has become one of the fastest-growing areas for tourism. What sets Marsa Alam apart is its untouched nature and coral reefs, which have not yet been heavily affected by crowds.

Each of these cities has its own personality: Hurghada is open and flexible, Sharm El-Sheikh is orderly and refined, and Marsa Alam is calm and natural. Tourists choose according to the kind of experience they are looking for, but in every case, they find beautiful seas, bright sunshine, and excellent service.

Diving, Nature Reserves, and the Beauty of Coral Reefs

The Red Sea is famous for its clear waters, which make diving there one of the best experiences in the world. Egypt's coral reefs are diverse, richly colored, and home to rare marine creatures.

Places such as Ras Mohammed, Abu Galum Reserve, Giftun Island, and the reefs near Marsa Alam have become extremely popular sites for divers. Some people come from the other side of the world just to take a dive in these waters.

Diving is not just a tourist activity; it also allows people to see another world under the sea. In some reefs, you may encounter pods of dolphins, sea turtles, or even certain species of sharks, all in a breathtaking natural setting.

There are also natural reserves around the Red Sea that are home to rare wildlife such as gazelles, foxes, and migratory birds. These reserves are not only for display but also play a key role in protecting the ecosystem.

Professional guides and divers also work to raise awareness among tourists not to touch the coral and not to throw waste into the sea, so that this environment can be preserved.

Tourism Expansion and Environmental Challenges

With the great success of Red Sea tourism came a large wave of urban and touristic expansion. Hotels, resorts, airports, roads, and electricity—massive projects were carried out to support the tourism sector.

But with this expansion, serious environmental problems began to appear. Coral reefs, which take hundreds of years to form, can be destroyed in moments by a poorly dropped anchor or an oil spill from a ship.

Unregulated construction and improper waste disposal have also affected water quality and marine life. In addition, expansions that encroach on reserves place pressure on the creatures that live there.

Because of this, initiatives were launched to protect the environment:

- NGOs began working with the state to enforce rules for diving and excursions.

- Beach and seabed cleanup campaigns were started.

- Tourism workers received training in environmentally friendly practices.

- Sustainable tourism was promoted—tourism that respects and protects the environment.

The government also began to enact laws to regulate urban expansion and monitor its environmental impact, especially in sensitive areas. There are ongoing efforts to strike a balance between economic benefit from tourism and preservation of natural resources.

The success of Red Sea tourism depends not only on services or natural beauty, but also on our ability to preserve the place so that it remains beautiful and safe for future generations.

Unit 10: Oases and Wonders

Famous Oases: Siwa, Dakhla, Kharga, Farafra

In the middle of the desert, far from the crowds and big cities, there is another world called the oases. Egypt's oases are not just a source of water in the heart of dryness; they are also places with a special character, a long history, and captivating natural beauty.

Among the most famous oases are Siwa, Dakhla, Kharga, and Farafra, and each of them has its own unique atmosphere and personality.

Siwa, for example, is located in the far west of Egypt, near the Libyan border. This oasis is famous for its unique culture and for its inhabitants, who speak Amazigh in addition to Arabic. It contains ancient temples, such as the Temple of Amun, as well as salt lakes, Cleopatra's Spring, and houses built from a material called kershef [a mixture of mud and salt]. Siwa is also well known for olive oil and dates.

Dakhla and Kharga are located in the New Valley and are considered among the most fertile oases. They have vast agricultural lands and villages with mud-brick houses decorated with beautiful wall paintings. Kharga also has Roman ruins and museums, and it serves as the administrative capital of the New Valley.

Farafra, the smallest and quietest, is close to the White Desert, and is known for its calm and serenity. Its population is small, but its natural setting is unique— especially at night, when the sky is adorned with an astonishing spread of stars.

Traditional Life in the Oases

Life in the oases has a different rhythm. People there live simply and are closely tied to nature and water. Agriculture is the foundation of life, especially the cultivation of palm trees, olives, grains, and vegetables.

People use traditional irrigation techniques, such as underground channels called foggara, which bring water from wells to fields with minimal waste.

Architecture in the oases is simple but functional. Houses are built from mud to keep the heat out in summer and preserve warmth in winter. These houses also carry a unique aesthetic touch, often decorated with drawings and ornaments inspired by the oasis heritage.

Hospitality is a very important part of life there. Visitors are always welcomed, and the first things offered are dates and tea. Communities are tightly knit, and the bonds between neighbors and families are strong.

Although technology has begun to enter the oases, there is still a strong desire to preserve traditions and customs. Festivals, folk songs, and traditional dances are passed down from generation to generation, especially during major occasions such as weddings or harvest season.

Geological Phenomena: Mountains, Caves, and Moving Sands

One of the features that makes Egypt's oases special is that they are not only green areas, but are also surrounded by stunning geological formations.

The White Desert, for example, near Farafra, is considered one of the strangest places in the world. The entire land there is covered with white limestone rocks, with wind-carved shapes that look like mushrooms or animals. The view there at night, under the moonlight, is enchanting.

There are also caves in areas such as Jabal al-Dakhla or Crystal Mountain. Sometimes these caves contain ancient carvings or primitive drawings, telling stories about the lives of early humans in the desert. Many geologists come to study them to learn more about the Earth's development.

Moving sands are also found in some areas around the oases. These are patches of very fine sand that are unstable underfoot. While not as dangerous as they are portrayed in movies, they can still be a trap if someone is not paying attention or walking without a guide.

The mountains surrounding the oases also play a role in shaping the climate and atmosphere, and they always provide a stunning backdrop to the oases—whether at sunrise or sunset.

Unit 11: Egypt's Official Governorates

Number of Governorates and Their Names

Egypt is administratively divided into 27 governorates, each with clear borders and a governor appointed to manage its affairs. This system of division is not new; since pharaonic times Egypt was divided into provinces, and the idea of administrative divisions has continued throughout the ages, adapting to political and economic circumstances.

The 27 governorates are: Cairo, Giza, Alexandria, Beheira, Kafr El Sheikh, Gharbia, Monufia, Dakahlia, Sharqia, Damietta, Port Said, Ismailia, Suez, North Sinai, South Sinai, Beni Suef, Fayoum, Minya, Assiut, Sohag, Qena, Luxor, Aswan, Red Sea, New Valley, and Matrouh.

Some governorates are enormous in area, such as the New Valley, which makes up more than 40% of Egypt's landmass but has very few inhabitants. Others are much smaller, such as Port Said or Damietta, yet have a much larger population.

How Are the Governorates Administered?

Each governorate is headed by a governor appointed by presidential decree. The governor supervises the implementation of government policies in areas such as education, healthcare, transport, housing, and more. They also oversee local administrations and make decisions that affect daily life in the governorate.

Alongside the governor, there are local councils, which are supposed to be elected by the people. Their role is to monitor services, discuss budgets, and participate in local decision-making. In practice, however, the role of these councils is sometimes limited, and they need stronger support in order to create a balance between central and local authority.

Governorates work in coordination with central ministries, which creates continuous links between Cairo and the regions. However, this can sometimes lead to slow implementation of projects or overlapping responsibilities, which causes problems on the ground.

Differences Between Urban and Rural Governorates

Not all governorates share the same character. Some are urban, such as Cairo, Alexandria, and Port Said, while others are rural or mixed, such as Monufia, Fayoum, and Sohag.

Urban governorates tend to have high population density, greater infrastructure, and more diverse services. Life there is fast-paced, and people are accustomed to using technology in their daily lives.

Rural governorates, by contrast, tend to be calmer, with economies that often rely on agriculture or small industries. Education and healthcare services may be less efficient or widespread, creating a gap between rural and urban areas.

There are also border governorates, such as North Sinai or Matrouh, which have their own unique nature because of security concerns, tribal structures, and different development challenges.

One of the major problems rural governorates face is internal migration, as many people leave villages to move to cities in search of better jobs or education.

Population and Services Distribution

The distribution of Egypt's population is highly unbalanced. About 95% of Egyptians live along a narrow strip surrounding the Nile Valley and Delta, with the rest spread across coastal cities, oases, and limited desert areas.

Areas like Cairo and Giza put enormous pressure on services because of rapid population growth, while other places have vast empty spaces but lack basic infrastructure.

Government services are not always distributed fairly. Schools, hospitals, and youth centers can be overcrowded in some governorates and scarce in others. Recently, the government has been trying to bring these services to underserved areas through initiatives such as Hayah Karima ("Decent Life"), which focuses on developing villages and infrastructure.

New technologies are also being used to better identify needs, such as geographic mapping and population data analysis, so that services are distributed based on accurate numbers rather than rough estimates.

Unit 12: Cultural and Informal Divisions

The Difference Between Official and Popular Divisions

Officially, Egypt is divided into 27 governorates, each with centers, cities, and villages. This division is administrative, used by the state to manage services, education, healthcare, and security. At the same time, however, people have another, informal division that they use in their speech and daily lives, which expresses their own sense of the identity of places.

People don't always say "Dakahlia Governorate," but instead say "from the Delta" or "I'm from Lower Egypt." In the south, you'll hear people say "I'm from Upper Egypt" or simply "from the south," without specifying a governorate.

This popular division is based on factors such as history, dialect, customs, types of agriculture, and even the landscape. So it's possible to find two areas within the same governorate whose people see themselves as very different in terms of culture and belonging.

The difference is not just in names; it also shows the complexity of Egyptian identity, which isn't limited to lines drawn on a map. Sometimes the popular division gives a more accurate reflection of people's relationship with their surroundings, which plays an important role in shaping social ties and identity.

Lower Egypt, Upper Egypt, and the Central Delta

Since ancient times, Egypt has been divided into two regions: Lower Egypt in the north and Upper Egypt in the south. The word baḥari means "near the sea," and qibli means "toward the qibla," or south.

Lower Egypt includes the governorates near the Mediterranean Sea, such as Alexandria, Beheira, Monufia, and others. These areas have fertile farmland, a large population, and cities with significant industrial and commercial activity.

Upper Egypt begins from Giza and extends down to Aswan, including governorates such as Beni Suef, Minya, Sohag, Qena, and Luxor. These regions are closer to traditional rural life, have a more conservative character, and agriculture there relies heavily on sugarcane, palm trees, and Nile farming.

The difference between the two regions is not only geographical but also cultural. In Lower Egypt, people often speak in lighter dialects and tend to be more socially open. In Upper Egypt, the dialect shows older Arabic features more clearly, and there is a stronger attachment to customs and traditions.

"Central Delta" is a term used for areas like Gharbia, Monufia, and Dakahlia, which lie between the two branches of the Nile: Damietta and Rosetta.

The differences among these regions are not only linguistic; they reflect people's special sense of belonging to their area, shaped by lifestyle, agriculture, and even patterns of social relations.

Nevertheless, people come together in times of celebration and crisis, and national identity unites them all, even if they express it in different ways.

Differences in Dialect, Customs, and Identity?

Yes, there are clear differences, though not always in the way people imagine. In terms of dialect, the Saʻidi dialect is noticeably different from those of Lower Egypt and Cairo. The differences appear in pronunciation and vocabulary, giving it a distinct local character. Even so, the dialects are largely understood by other Egyptians, especially since many Saʻidis adjust their speech when dealing with people from outside Upper Egypt.

As for customs, people in Upper Egypt tend to hold on to traditions more strongly—whether in clothing, food, neighborly relations, or celebrating occasions. In Lower Egypt, there is generally more flexibility, especially in large cities.

When it comes to identity, many people in Upper Egypt feel they have a distinctiveness, rooted in a long history of pride and struggle. In Lower Egypt, people sometimes emphasize openness and diversity, particularly in port cities and commercial hubs.

But despite these differences, there is a strong thread that binds all Egyptians: belonging to the homeland, love for the Nile, and a shared history. This is what makes Egypt unique—united in its diversity.

Podcasts

Unit 1: An Overview of Egypt

- Welcome everyone. Today we're going to talk about the geography of Egypt—a fascinating and important topic. We've got an article that breaks it down clearly.

- Welcome! And yes, it's definitely a subject worth discussing. Egypt's geography has so many details.

- Let's start with the first thing: Egypt's location. The article describes it as strategic.

- Exactly. Just the idea of it being in the middle between three continents—Africa, Asia, and Europe—that alone is huge.

- And besides that, it overlooks two important seas, the Mediterranean and the Red Sea. That gives it a completely different status.

- Of course, of course. And that brings us to another very important point the article mentioned.

- The Suez Canal.

- That's it. The Suez Canal isn't just a waterway—it practically changed global trade.

- Absolutely. It connected East and West in a direct, fast way. That location, together with the canal, means Egypt is always at the heart of world events.

- Exactly. And that same location also defines Egypt's borders to a large extent.

- Ah, yes—the borders.

- Egypt has two kinds, really. If we look, we'll find clear natural borders—

- Like the Mediterranean in the north and the Red Sea in the east.

- And the other kind are political borders.

- Like with Sudan and Libya, for example.

- Yes. Those are mostly lines drawn right through the desert as a result of agreements—not natural barriers like the sea.

- So they're completely different in nature from the coastal borders.
- Totally. The dynamics there are completely different.
- Alright, let's move inside the country. The article talks about 27 governorates—that's the administrative division, right?
- Right. And that reflects the huge diversity within Egypt itself.
- Of course. Life in crowded Cairo is completely different from quiet Aswan, or from a frontier governorate in the desert. Each has its own character.
- Exactly.
- And then there's the other division we often hear about—Lower Egypt and Upper Egypt. The article talks about the Sa'id (Upper Egypt).
- Yes, Upper Egypt is not just a geographic label for southern Egypt—it also carries deep historical and cultural weight tied to that region.
- So it's not just a word.
- Not at all. It has real significance.
- And that diversity must also show in the climate.
- Of course. Overall, Egypt is a desert country—dry, with sun almost all year round and very little rain.
- But there must be differences between Alexandria and Aswan, for example.
- Of course. On the northern coasts, the Mediterranean makes the weather milder, especially in winter. But the farther inland or south you go, the hotter and drier it gets.
- And that's tied to terrain too, isn't it?
- Very much so. Egypt's terrain is strikingly varied. The most important feature, of course, is the Nile Valley.
- That narrow green strip where most of us live.
- Exactly. And alongside it are the Eastern Desert, with its rocky mountains along the Red Sea, and the vast Western Desert with its oases. And then there's Sinai with its high mountains.
- That mix is what determined where people could live throughout history.
- Exactly.
- And now we come to maybe the most important point: the Nile. The article calls it the "lifeline."

- And that's probably the most accurate description. Honestly, it's hard to even imagine Egypt without the Nile.

- The article gives a figure I remember well: about 95% of Egyptians live along the Nile.

- An astonishing number.

- In that narrow strip of the Valley, or in the Delta above. It's an incredible concentration of people.

- Which shows how total the dependence on it is—not just for water and farming.

- Of course not. It's also transport, fishing, and part of our very identity and culture.

- Exactly. And in the Nile's modern history, there's a key point the article refers to.

- You mean the High Dam.

- Yes, the High Dam in Aswan. It was a huge turning point—controlling the floods, generating lots of electricity, and helping expand agriculture. Tremendous benefits.

- But of course it had another side.

- Yes. Any project of that scale has consequences. The main one was trapping the silt.

- The same silt that used to fertilize the land every year.

- Exactly. That silt was the natural fertilizer of the Nile Valley. When it was held back behind the dam, soil fertility was affected in the long run.

- And then there were other consequences, like the displacement of the Nubian people.

- Yes, that was a huge story, with major social and human costs. So the dam had two sides.

- Gains and challenges at the same time.

- Exactly. And that shows just how sensitive and complex managing the Nile's resources is.

- And despite everything, the Nile is still the foundation.

- It is, and it will remain the foundation. Egypt's future is deeply tied to it.

- So this quick tour, inspired by the article, shows us how all these factors interact: location, borders, terrain, climate—and above all, the Nile.

- o Together they shaped the Egypt we know. And maybe that leads us to a question for the future.

- o Go ahead.

- o With all the challenges we keep hearing about—climate change, population pressure, the regional water situation—and with the Nile still being the lifeline, how might Egypt's relationship with the Nile need to change or evolve in the coming years?

- o A very important question, and one that really requires thought. So with that, we've come to the end of our talk today about Egypt's geography. Thank you so much for your time.

- o The thanks are mine.

Unit 2: The Nile and Society

- o Welcome everyone. Today we'll be talking about something that touches the lives of almost every Egyptian: the Nile River.

- o Of course, the Nile is a whole different story.

- o Exactly. We have an article to go through that paints a picture of the Nile's central role in agriculture, in transport—both in the past and today—and how things have changed. Maybe the most important point to start with is the extreme concentration of the population around it.

- o That's a fact that's a bit shocking if you stop and think about it. More than 90% of Egypt's population is crowded into a very small strip along the Nile and its Delta.

- o Which we call the Nile Valley and Delta.

- o Right. Altogether, this area makes up less than 5% of Egypt's total land. That fact alone shows how much the Nile really is the lifeline.

- o Let's explain clearly what the Valley and Delta are. The Valley is that long green strip running from Aswan up to Cairo—farmland right in the middle of the desert.

- o Correct. Then north of Cairo, the Nile branches out like a tree, forming the big green triangle of the Nile Delta that empties into the sea. It's a very rich agricultural region. But houses and buildings are eating into the farmland itself, reducing that fertile land. And especially in the areas closer to the sea, there's another problem: soil salinity.

- o Right, the salt content in the soil is increasing.

- Exactly. And that, of course, makes farming harder and requires costly special treatments. The Valley is also under pressure, with expanding cities and growing demand for resources.

- And when we talk about the Nile and land, we have to talk about farming. In the old days, things were very different. There was the silt.

- Oh, the silt was a real treasure. Those were the deposits the Nile brought with the annual flood, nourishing the soil and making it incredibly fertile for farmers.

- And that's what gave Egyptian wheat, cotton, and so on their reputation.

- Exactly. But all of that changed after the High Dam in the 1960s. It saved the country from floods that used to drown everything and stored huge amounts of water, but it also trapped the silt behind it.

- In Lake Nasser.

- Yes. So the direct result was a drop in the soil's natural fertility. Farmers had to rely heavily on chemical fertilizers to make up for the loss.

- And fertilizers come at a cost. Over time, with water sometimes not being enough, new irrigation systems appeared, like sprinklers and drip irrigation.

- Exactly, to save as much water as possible. It's all interconnected.

- Alright, that's agriculture and water. The Nile was also an important transport route, right? The article really highlighted that. River transport used to be the main way people and goods moved around.

- What happened?

- Well, with new roads, trains, and railways, its role has really diminished. But it hasn't disappeared. In the south, for example, Nile cruises between Luxor and Aswan are still very famous, and heavy goods are sometimes transported by river.

- And there's talk of reviving it again.

- Yes, there are efforts and discussions, especially since it could be cheaper and cleaner than road transport and could ease traffic and pollution a bit. So there's still hope.

- Now we come to maybe the key point in the Nile's modern history: the High Dam. The article describes it as a massive national project.

- It really was a gigantic project by every measure, and it completely changed Egyptians' relationship with the Nile. It had a lot of benefits, of course.

- o   Like what? What were the most important ones?

- o   The most important was that it protected Egypt from the danger of annual flooding, which used to be disastrous. It also stored a huge amount of water in Lake Nasser—

- o   The biggest man-made lake at the time.

- o   Exactly. That allowed year-round irrigation, agricultural expansion, and of course the generation of electricity, which was a major breakthrough at the time.

- o   But nothing comes with only positives. Surely there were also challenges or downsides.

- o   Of course. As we said, the dam trapped the silt, which affected soil fertility and fish in the Nile, and the ecosystem itself changed.

- o   And new challenges appeared afterward too.

- o   Exactly. Water management itself became harder with the huge increase in population and rising demands. And then there's the regional dimension—the dam projects being built in upstream countries.

- o   Yes, and that makes the issue of water very sensitive and very complicated.

- o   Extremely. A big, ongoing challenge for Egypt.

- o   So the story of the Nile, as the article explains, is one of constant interaction: nature shaping people's lives, then humans intervening strongly—like with the High Dam—and creating a whole new reality.

- o   That's exactly it. And looking ahead, we have to keep all this in mind. Sure, we built the dam, but the Nile is still affected by many other factors.

- o   Like what?

- o   Like population growth that never stops, climate change that could affect the amount of water reaching Egypt in the first place, and of course politics and disputes between the Nile Basin countries.

- o   The issue is really intertwined.

- o   Very much so. And that makes us ask: are engineering solutions like dams enough for the future, or do we need to think of completely different solutions? Maybe changing the way we consume water or using new technologies—to make sure the Nile continues playing its vital role for generations to come. That's a very big, open question.

- o

Unit 3: The Desert Is Not Just Sand

- Today we're going to talk about something that many people have a rather stereotypical idea about: Egypt's deserts. As soon as we say "desert," the picture that comes to mind is endless yellow sand.

- Yes, exactly.

- But the truth, as an article we read explains, is that Egypt's deserts are a whole other world—much more complex, full of diversity, history, and life.

- That picture really does them an injustice. They're not just empty space.

- Exactly. Today we'll focus on the main parts: the Western Desert, the Eastern Desert, and the treasures between them—the oases. We want to understand their nature, their importance, and their challenges too.

- Right. Each region has its own character—geologically, economically, culturally. And the most fascinating part is how humans managed to adapt and live in these environments for thousands of years, right up to today.

- So let's start with the big one: the Western Desert. Its area is huge—about two-thirds of Egypt.

- Almost, yes.

- And it's not just flat land. It has mountains, and enormous sandy stretches like the Great Sand Sea, with dunes that shift shapes and rise high, like an open-air geological museum. There are rare sights, like the Crystal Mountain with its glittering formations, sparkling as if jewels had sprung from the ground.

- Amazing.

- And another unique feature: the White Desert, with its white formations shaped by erosion over millions of years. It's a breathtaking landscape, made up of remains of ancient marine life.

- And of course, the area has historical importance too, especially in World War II and the battles of El Alamein.

- Absolutely.

- And now there's talk of new uses: agricultural expansion, big solar energy projects, and new roads linking it with the Valley and Delta.

- Yes, there's clear development going on. Alright, if we move to the other side—the Eastern Desert, between the Nile and the Red Sea—its nature is a bit different.

- Different how?

- Its terrain is mountainous, very rugged, with the high ranges of the Red Sea mountains.

- And what sets it apart besides the mountains?

- Well, its main distinction historically and economically is minerals. Since pharaonic times, it's been a source of gold, copper, and other resources.

- And still is today.

- Yes, mining and exploration are still active. And, of course, it's Egypt's gateway to the Red Sea, with important trading ports.

- And it also has natural treasures like Wadi el-Gemal Nature Reserve, which protects rare wildlife.

- Very beautiful.

- It's also home to long-standing Bedouin tribes, like the Ababda and the Bishari, with their own culture and traditions tied to the land.

- And there's also development happening there: industrial zones, new roads, and so on.

- Of course, the state is trying to strengthen its economic role.

- Alright, and from the deserts we move to the green hearts within them—the oases. Like you said, gems in the sand: Siwa, Bahariya, Dakhla, Kharga, Farafra. Each has its own character. Siwa, for example, with its distinct Amazigh heritage and landmarks like the remains of the Temple of Amun.

- The famous Temple of Amun.

- Exactly. It had major religious importance in the past.

- So what do the oases live on, basically? What's the secret behind that green in the middle of yellow?

- The whole secret is groundwater. That's the main source of life there, surfacing as springs or wells. That's why agriculture is the backbone of their economy—date palms, olives, vegetables.

- So it's not just farming, is it?

- No, of course not. They're also cultural and historical centers. And recently, they've drawn attention as destinations for eco-tourism—for

- people who want to enjoy nature and local culture responsibly—as well as therapeutic tourism.

- But there must be challenges too.

- Of course. The biggest is the pressure on limited groundwater. Climate change also has an effect. And many young people migrate to cities looking for better opportunities.

- Which brings us to life in the desert itself. It's certainly not easy.

- Very tough. It requires patience and endurance. The Bedouins, the original inhabitants, developed a certain lifestyle over centuries, relying on moving with resources.

- And that lifestyle has started to change.

- Yes, it has. With some services reaching these areas, more settled villages have appeared. But there are still problems: isolation, lack of opportunities, climate change, and migration to cities—all of which threaten local cultures.

- Yet despite the difficulties, these deserts represent major opportunities for the future, especially in sustainable development.

- Exactly. There's potential for clean tourism, renewable energy, modern farming methods that don't use much water. They're not just empty sand.

- Exactly. The picture is much clearer now. Egypt's deserts are a rich and complex world—full of history, geology, life, opportunities, and big challenges too.

- And maybe one last point to leave us thinking: the values the desert can teach us—patience, self-reliance, simplicity.

- A really important question: do those values still have a place in our fast, complicated world?

- A question truly worth reflecting on.

Unit 4: The Seas and the Coasts

- Welcome everyone. Today we're going to talk about a very interesting topic based on the material we have: Egypt's coasts on the Mediterranean and the Red Sea. The text we're looking at shows just how important these coasts are—geographically, economically, and environmentally. We'll try to go through its main points.

- Exactly. And they really are vital coasts—not just beaches. They've always played a big role in people's lives and in Egypt's development.

- Alright, let's start with the northern coast on the Mediterranean. The text says it's about 1,000 km long. That's a huge distance.

- Of course, not small at all. And along that stretch are very important cities like Alexandria, Port Said, and Damietta.

- And those cities aren't just ports, right? The text says they're also commercial and cultural centers.

- Exactly. Take Alexandria, for example. It's a clear model, with its long history linking different eras and civilizations. But maybe the most distinctive feature of this whole coast, as the text points out, is the moderate climate—the pleasant weather most of the year.

- And what did that help with, apart from people wanting to live there?

- It supported other important things. Yes, stable settlement is one, but also agriculture. Certain crops—like olives and figs—thrive in that climate. And maybe most importantly, the northern coast became the main summer resort for Egyptians for a very long time. Domestic summer tourism was centered there.

- True, the northern coast is tied in all our minds with summer and vacations. But recently the text draws attention to another point: the rapid pace of urban development. Can you explain that a bit?

- Urban development here means the big wave of building and expansion happening—new tourist villages, resorts, and lots of new buildings all along the coast.

- Ah, I see.

- Of course, that has economic benefits, but it also sparked a big debate: what effect does this have on the coastal environment, on the beaches themselves?

- So it's a controversial issue.

- Definitely. Are we building too much? Is this changing the coast forever? These are important questions.

- Okay, let's move now to the eastern coast on the Red Sea. What's the most distinctive thing about it, according to the text?

- The Red Sea is a bit different. Population density there is much lower than on the Mediterranean, but its reputation in tourism is global.

- Like which cities, for example?

- Cities like Hurghada, Sharm el-Sheikh, Marsa Alam, and also Ain Sokhna. These names are well-known to tourists all over the world.

- And the text highlights a major attraction there.

- Of course—the coral reefs. They're rare natural treasures, found in abundance in the Red Sea. Their colors and formations are truly stunning, and that's what makes the region one of the world's top diving destinations. Diving there is a whole other experience—an underwater world full of amazing life and biodiversity.

- So biodiversity is the defining feature there.

- It's a major feature, and a huge tourist draw. But the Red Sea also has another big importance: maritime trade. Ports like Safaga and Suez serve trade routes, especially with the Gulf and Asia, and being close to the Suez Canal doubles its importance.

- A strategic location, in other words.

- Exactly. That waterway connects the whole world, and this coast is part of that big picture.

- The text also mentioned another use of the region beyond tourism and trade.

- Yes, it pointed out renewable energy projects—solar and wind power. The conditions there are ideal for such projects: strong sun and open areas with steady wind.

- But despite all that potential, there must be challenges.

- Of course. The biggest challenge is the heavy pressure tourism itself puts on the sensitive environment—especially the coral reefs.

- Sensitive how?

- They're extremely sensitive to any change in water quality or temperature. Climate change or pollution can destroy them easily. That's why protecting them is very difficult and requires a lot of effort and careful planning.

- That makes us ask about traditional activities like fishing. Do they still exist and play an important role on these coasts? The text mentioned that too.

- Yes, absolutely. Fishing is still considered a traditional occupation, passed down in many coastal communities—like Rashid and Damietta on the Mediterranean, and Suez and other towns on the Red Sea. Fishermen's lives are directly tied to the sea, to fishing seasons when certain fish are abundant, and of course to weather conditions that determine when they can go out.

- And has the profession stayed the same, or has it changed?

o It's evolved. There are still traditional methods, but there's also newer equipment and bigger boats. That can increase catches, but it can also put more pressure on fish stocks if there's no regulation. And if we return to trade and tourism more broadly—

o Maritime trade, as we said, is a backbone. The big ports—Alexandria, Port Said, Suez—are Egypt's gateways to the world. And of course, the Suez Canal is the most important piece of this whole system.

o And sea tourism itself?

o That's developing too. It's not just beaches and diving anymore. Now there's interest in yacht trips and large cruise ships. That requires specific facilities at tourist ports to welcome them.

o All of this underscores the importance of these coasts. But the text ends with a note of caution about the future.

o Exactly. There are clear efforts to improve the infrastructure—expanding ports, building new corniches, new tourist areas. But the biggest challenge is how to create a balance.

o Balance between what and what?

o Between development and preservation. The threat of marine pollution is very serious, coming from many sources—industrial discharge, ship traffic. And it doesn't just harm marine life like fish and coral. It can reach us too, affecting our health.

o So the future requires very careful planning.

o Exactly. These coasts have always been a source of livelihood, life, and inspiration for Egyptians. For them to remain that way, future planning has to be smart, balancing economic development and job opportunities with protecting these natural treasures for future generations. It's a difficult equation, but a necessary one.

o So that gives us an overview of the main points the text raised about Egypt's Mediterranean and Red Sea coasts. We saw how each has its own character, but both are hugely important for Egypt—economically, culturally, environmentally.

o And the big question for the future—and it's a very important one—is this: with all these pressures from development and expansion, and with the challenges of climate change affecting seas around the world, what new and innovative ways can Egypt adopt to ensure its coasts remain a source of life and prosperity—but in a sustainable way? That's a major challenge, and one that requires constant thought and work.

Unit 5: Greater Cairo

- Welcome everyone. Today we're going to talk about Cairo—but not just in a general way. Cairo is really a story all of its own.

- Absolutely. It's a city that's over a thousand years old, and when we read about it, we're always discovering new sides to it.

- Exactly. It's not just an administrative capital, that's for sure.

- Not at all. If we look at its history, it began with Fustat, in the time of Amr ibn al-'As.

- And then came Fatimid Cairo in the 10th century, along with Al-Azhar, which was built then.

- Right. And it kept developing—Mamluks, Ottomans—each era left its mark, layers stacked one on top of another.

- And in more recent history, Khedive Ismail's attempt to make it like Paris also shaped a large part of it.

- True, and that brings us to the idea of "Greater Cairo."

- Yes, that's an important point. It's not just Cairo Governorate within its borders.

- Not at all. It's much larger—that's what they call the urban agglomeration, which includes Cairo, Giza, and Qalyubia.

- Giza, west of the Nile—of course with the pyramids and the Sphinx—but also with very modern residential areas like Dokki and Mohandessin.

- A strange mix, really, between history and modernity. And Qalyubia, in the north, has industry—like Shubra El-Kheima, for example.

- And it's also the gateway to the Delta.

- And what matters more than the administrative divisions is that people's lives in these three governorates are deeply interconnected on a daily basis—work, errands, transportation.

- Millions moving back and forth every day. And that brings us to the biggest challenge—something anyone who lives in or has visited Cairo knows: traffic.

- Mm, the traffic is a whole story of its own. We're talking about more than 20 million people living and moving around this area.

- An unbelievable amount of pressure on everything, especially transport and infrastructure.

- And of course, with that growth and the migration from rural areas to the city in the past, informal housing appeared—the "ashwa'iyyat" (slums). True, the state is now trying to improve these areas, and we've seen projects like Al-Asmarat and Bashayer al-Kheir.

- Yes, big efforts are being made. But the phenomenon still reflects the roots of the city's rapid growth.

- And at the same time, we see huge projects like the New Administrative Capital.

- Exactly. The stated goal is to ease the pressure on old Cairo and redistribute population and institutions.

- So, in a way, it's an attempt to redraw the demographic and administrative map.

- More or less, yes. But aside from all these challenges and projects, Cairo still remains the country's cultural and administrative center.

- Of course—all the state institutions are there: the presidency, the parliament, the ministries.

- And beyond that, it's the heart of Egyptian and Arab media—television, radio, major newspapers, publishing houses.

- And cultural and artistic life too— cinemas, the Cairo Opera House, important museums like the Egyptian Museum and the Museum of Civilization.

- And we can't forget the major universities—Cairo University, Al-Azhar.

- And despite all the difficulties—even the traffic that can sometimes make you hate life—

- Mm, true.

- It still has a unique spirit you just can't find anywhere else.

- Exactly. The small details: the voices of street vendors, the smell of food in the alleys, people's stories in the cafés—that's the spirit of Cairo.

- It's a city that honestly isn't easy—it can be exhausting.

- Yes, very exhausting at times.

- But at the same time, you could never replace it. It has its own special magic.

- Exactly. And that maybe brings us to a final question: with all this massive expansion and new urban projects like the New Administrative

Capital, how can Greater Cairo—with all its rich history—preserve its spirit and identity amid all these changes?

- o A very important question, and one that really needs thought—how that balance can be achieved.

Unit 6: The Delta and Its Treasures

- o Welcome everyone. Today we're going to talk about a very vital region in Egypt—its beating heart of agriculture and history: the Nile Delta.
- o Oh, absolutely.
- o It's a huge, wide expanse stretching from north of Cairo all the way to the Mediterranean—fertile land with a very special character.
- o Exactly. And the Delta isn't just farmland—it's a whole world of its own.
- o A world indeed.
- o It has important governorates, like Dakahlia with its capital Mansoura, Gharbia with Tanta, and Sharqia with Zagazig as its capital.
- o Mm.
- o And each one has its own personality and economic activity. So today we can explore life there a bit, and some treasures not everyone knows about.
- o Great idea. Let's start with those major governorates you mentioned. Dakahlia, with Mansoura as its capital—the article we're looking at describes it as an important center of knowledge and culture.
- o Right. Not just an administrative capital.
- o Of course not. And in Gharbia, the most famous thing is Tanta and the mosque of al-Sayyid al-Badawi.
- o Yes, al-Sayyid al-Badawi is a major religious figure, and his annual mawlid is a massive event every year.
- o And there are traditional industries there too.
- o And Zagazig, the capital of Sharqia, has strong commercial activity closely tied to agriculture.
- o Exactly. And maybe that's what highlights the Delta's greatest importance—it's really Egypt's breadbasket.
- o That's the perfect description. Its alluvial soil, carried by the Nile, is among the most fertile in the world.

- Amazing.
- It produces essential crops we can't do without: wheat, rice, and of course cotton—world-famous Egyptian cotton.
- And here comes the role of the fellahin, the farmers. The article talks about them not just as agricultural workers.
- Of course not. They're another story entirely—people with deeply inherited expertise, passed down through generations. They know the land, the water, the seasons. Farming is their heritage.
- That knowledge is a treasure in itself. But the article also says there's now a move toward modernization—new irrigation methods, different seeds. And that raises an important question:
- Does that create a kind of conflict between the old and the new?
- Well, modernization is definitely needed to face challenges like population growth or water shortages. But at the same time, preserving the traditional wisdom of the fellahin is important too.
- Because it's adapted to the nature of the land.
- Exactly—adapted to our soil and climate. The balance isn't easy, but it's necessary. And agriculture there supports many other industries in the Delta.
- Like what, for example?
- Plenty of food industries—factories that package vegetables and fruit, dairies and dairy products.
- Mm.
- And of course the textile industry, based above all on our high-quality Egyptian cotton.
- But maybe the most prominent and world-famous is the furniture industry in Damietta, right?
- Oh yes, Damietta is in a league of its own. The article describes it as a "city of workshops," where nearly every household has a skilled craftsman. Master artisans, inheriting the craft generation after generation. Their work is famous throughout the Middle East and beyond.
- And Damietta is one of those treasures that maybe doesn't get as much media attention as Mansoura or Tanta.
- True—and there are many other towns and villages with their own importance. Take Kafr el-Sheikh, for example—it has Lake Burullus.

This is Egypt... The Geography of Egypt | 119

- Ah yes, a natural reserve.

- Exactly. A key spot for migratory birds, and a whole community lives there on fishing and lake life.

- Beautiful.

- And there are still villages preserving very old handicrafts—like handmade carpets with their vibrant colors and designs.

- And pottery too.

- Of course. Pottery made from the local clay, and also copperwork, palm-leaf weaving. These aren't just industries—they're part of the identity and history of the region.

- And when we talk about identity, food has to come up. The article mentioned fiteer meshaltet and gebna adeema.

- Of course. And let's not forget fesikh.

- Fesikh is tied to a certain occasion, right?

- Exactly—it's mainly linked to Sham el-Nessim. It's salted, fermented fish, prepared in a very special way, hugely popular in the Delta and across Egypt. Foods like this show how deeply people are connected to their land, their seasons, and traditional preservation methods.

- So the picture we're painting of the Delta is really beautiful—land of abundance, skilled people, unique cultural life. But the article doesn't ignore the challenges.

- Of course not. And that's an important point. The biggest, most dangerous challenge is the loss of farmland.

- Because of construction on it.

- Exactly. Urban sprawl and building on fertile land is a huge threat. And there's another problem too: increasing soil salinity, especially near the northern coasts. That may be linked to climate change—or to the effects of the High Dam.

- It could be either—or both. The causes are intertwined. But the result is real risks threatening the Delta's very existence as a productive agricultural region.

- So the Delta, with all its treasures—its agricultural, industrial, and cultural history—is facing big challenges for the future.

- Exactly. And that brings us to an important question we need to think about after reading and discussing this article.

- o Go ahead.
- o With all these pressures—development, population growth, environmental challenges like land loss—how can we achieve the difficult balance? How can we preserve Egypt's agricultural heart and the Delta's unique cultural identity, along with people's traditional livelihoods like farming, pottery, and furniture-making, while also allowing for the development people need?
- o It's a very tough question. And that balance really is the greatest challenge.

Unit 7: Upper Egypt: The South that is Up

- o Welcome everyone. Today we want to explore together a region in Egypt that has a special charm and a long history—Upper Egypt, or as people call it, Wagh Qibli. Our discussion is based on an interesting text we read that gives us a good glimpse of life there. The first thing that caught my attention in the text is how Upper Egypt itself is divided.
- o Exactly. The text explains that there are two main parts: Lower Upper Egypt, which is the northern section closer to the Delta and Cairo, including governorates like Fayoum, Beni Suef, and Minya.
- o Right.
- o And then Upper Upper Egypt, also called al-Sa'id al-Gawwani, which is the southern part stretching from Asyut down to Aswan. And what struck me is that the word "upper" here doesn't mean north or south geographically—it refers to actual elevation above sea level.
- o So, based on this division, what are the key differences the text highlights between the two areas?
- o Geographically, life in Upper Egypt in general, as the text describes, is concentrated in a very narrow strip along the Nile. As soon as you move a little away, you hit desert immediately.
- o True.
- o But the differences do exist. Lower Upper Egypt, being closer to the capital, is more influenced by it and is strongly agricultural in character. Upper Upper Egypt is noted in the text for having tighter social bonds and a stronger attachment to inherited traditions.
- o That makes sense.
- o And maybe that partly comes from historical and geographical factors that kept it relatively more isolated. The text talks a lot about this idea of

tribal ties—meaning the importance of family and tribe in organizing life and relationships there. Life in the villages, as described, has a real collective spirit.

o   Exactly.

o   But at the same time, it's clear that things are changing.

o   For sure. The text points to major forces of change: technology reaching almost everywhere, education spreading far more than before, and the phenomenon of internal migration—that's the term used for the movement of many people, especially young men, from Upper Egypt to the big cities.

o   Like Cairo and Alexandria.

o   Exactly. They go looking for better job opportunities. And all these factors are shifting ideas and lifestyles.

o   And that also shows in the role of women, whose participation in education and work has grown, and maybe this sometimes creates a kind of push and pull between generations or between older traditions and newer ideas young people are exposed to.

o   Yes, change is real, but it doesn't come without challenges. The text is clear about that too—it points to problems still present, especially in rural villages.

o   Like what, for example?

o   For instance, weak infrastructure—a term that covers lots of basic services: quality of roads, equipped hospitals, sanitation, access to clean water. All these are essential for a good life.

o   Right.

o   And the lack of job opportunities remains a big challenge, which is part of what drives internal migration. But on the positive side, awareness is rising. People are more willing to demand their rights and take steps to improve their communities themselves.

o   And when we think about Upper Egypt, we find that each city has its own unique character. The text gives important examples: Asyut, for instance, is described as a cultural and educational center in the heart of Upper Egypt, with a major university.

o   Yes. And Sohag is described as a somewhat quieter city with important religious and historical sites.

o   And Qena?

- It is known for traditional industries and handicrafts, and it has a key location linking different areas. And of course, Luxor is something else altogether. The text ties its glorious Pharaonic history and unmatched monuments—like Deir el-Bahari, the mortuary temple of Queen Hatshepsut, a stunning site on the west bank—

- Truly a masterpiece.

- —and its attempts today to position itself as a modern tourist city. Finally, Aswan, with its unique beauty, as Egypt's southern gateway to Africa, with its rich cultural diversity, especially the Nubian culture.

- Yes, the text devoted important attention to Nubia.

- Exactly. Nubia, south of Aswan, has a culture, language, and traditions that are very distinctive and different from the rest of Upper Egypt. Their history is ancient, with strong ties to Pharaonic Egypt.

- And the text points out a major challenge they faced.

- Yes, the greatest challenge was the building of the High Dam in the 1960s, which unfortunately flooded their original villages and forced them to relocate.

- A very difficult experience for sure, and despite all of that, the text shows that they are determined to preserve the Nubian identity. This expresses their strong sense of belonging to their heritage, their language, and these unique traditions of theirs.

- Exactly, and there are ongoing efforts to preserve it. This Nubian identity is an authentic and very rich part of the mosaic of cultural diversity that characterizes all of Egypt.

- So, Upper Egypt is a complex and diverse world—not just one uniform place. There's a huge gradation and variety from north to south, in geography and in social and cultural life. And that brings us to an important question: given the reality that the text portrays, how will Upper Egypt manage this difficult balancing act? How will it preserve its deep roots and rich traditions, while also adapting—and it must adapt—to new opportunities of the modern era? The answer to that question is what will shape the future of Upper Egypt and its identity in the years ahead.

Unit 8: The Suez Canal and Sinai

- Welcome everyone. Today we'll talk about two topics that are extremely important for Egypt and the whole region: the Suez Canal and Sinai.

They're not just pieces of geography—they're central parts of Egypt's history and present.

- o Welcome! Exactly, and that's what the article we're looking at today tries to show: how the Canal, as a global trade artery, is a vital route for the movement of goods and ships between East and West, and how Sinai, with its size, history, and natural character, has shaped Egypt's economic and political identity.

- o So let's start with the Suez Canal. It's obviously much more than just a waterway connecting the Red Sea to the Mediterranean. From the moment it opened in 1869, it completely changed the map of world trade.

- o Of course. It cut down distances and time dramatically, and that importance always kept it at the center of major events. One pivotal moment we remember is the nationalization in 1956.

- o Yes, President Abdel Nasser's decision at the time.

- o Exactly. Making the canal fully Egyptian-run was a hugely important declaration of sovereignty. But at the same time, it triggered an international crisis—the Tripartite Aggression.

- o The attack by Britain, France, and Israel. Exactly.

- o Right. That shows you how the Canal has always been, and still is, a highly sensitive strategic point worldwide.

- o And in more recent history, in 2015, there was the New Suez Canal project. The goal was to increase its capacity, right?

- o Yes, so that more ships could pass at the same time and waiting periods would be reduced. The aim was clearly economic—increasing Egypt's revenue.

- o And that revenue is already massive, in foreign currency.

- o Of course. It's a very important source. But as the article points out, the Canal's importance isn't just financial. It also gives Egypt significant political weight in its international relations—it's a powerful card to hold.

- o Got it. Now let's turn to the cities along the Canal itself. Suez in the south has a famous history of resistance, Ismailia in the center is calmer and the headquarters of the Canal Authority, and Port Said in the north has a special status. The article describes Port Said as once being considered an "international city."

- o International in what sense?

- It meant there were many different nationalities and cultures, especially during the foreign administration of the Canal before nationalization. That left a lasting impact on its architecture and culture. And of course, all of these cities' residents have lives tied directly to the Canal—their work and daily life revolve around it.

- Exactly. Okay, now if we leave the Canal and head east, we reach Sinai. This peninsula holds a very special place in Egyptians' hearts, and its natural environment is unique.

- Of course, the diversity there is stunning: high mountains in the south, like Saint Catherine, vast desert in the center, and beaches like Dahab and Sharm el-Sheikh, world-famous for their coral reefs and diving.

- A diver's paradise, as they say.

- Exactly. And the article also points out that Sinai isn't only about tourism. It also has important natural and mineral resources, and it talks about the indigenous Bedouin people, who have a very distinctive culture and traditions closely tied to the land and the desert and mountain environment.

- Their deep knowledge of the land is really remarkable.

- Definitely. And historically, Sinai has seen many difficult times and wars. The most important modern event, of course, is the October War of 1973.

- Of course—the war of liberation and the recovery of the land.

- Exactly. That's a hugely significant national occasion tied to Sinai. And in more recent years, there have been other challenges, as the article hints—security challenges, with the presence of armed groups.

- Yes, that was worrying for a time.

- Of course. The state responded with security operations to confront that, but at the same time—and this is very important—there has been a major focus on large-scale national development projects there.

- You mean the new roads, hospitals, and big projects we keep hearing about?

- Exactly. Strong infrastructure, investments, and attempts to link Sinai more deeply to the rest of Egypt, achieving real development. The goal is stability and development together.

- And that also strengthens the sense that Sinai is an inseparable part of the homeland—not only a land with historic and religious significance, but also a place with a future and opportunities.

- Absolutely. So when we look at the full picture the article presents, we see how the Canal with its cities, and Sinai with its nature, history, and people, all form one integrated whole. They carry huge strategic, economic, symbolic, and emotional importance for Egypt.

- And with all these efforts in development and in facing challenges, the open question for the future is: what will the next chapter be in the story of Sinai and its relationship with Egypt?

- That's an important question—and one that always keeps us thinking about the future.

Unit 9: The Red Sea and Beach Tourism

- Welcome everyone. Today we've got a very enjoyable topic—we're going to talk about a magical place in Egypt: the Red Sea coast. We read an article about it, designed for learners of Egyptian Arabic, and it gives a really nice picture of this region—its cities, its natural beauty, and also the challenges it faces. Let's take a look at the main points. First of all, this coast is long—it stretches from Suez all the way down to the Sudanese border. The article explains how the area has become a world-famous tourist destination. Let's start with Hurghada. The text says it was originally just a fishing village.

- Yes, a very simple fishing village—a tiny place where people depended entirely on fishing.

- Imagine the scale of the change!

- It's incredible. Starting in the 1980s it transformed into a large, open tourist city. That's really its character—practical, fast-growing. But then you have Sharm el-Sheikh. The text described it as the "jewel of tourism."

- Hmm, why that phrase? Did the article explain a particular difference?

- I think the idea is that planning and design there were different—more attention to detail, a very high level of tourist services.

- Like hotels and restaurants and so on.

- Exactly. Everything is built to a high standard, which made it suitable to host major international conferences and events. That gave it a more organized, polished identity.

- Then there's Marsa Alam—that's the newest, right? The text says its environment is still pristine, with coral reefs less affected by overcrowding.

o Right. Maybe because its development is more recent, the focus there has been on calm and closeness to nature.

o So it's a slightly different experience.

o Yes, an experience for people looking for more relaxation, especially diving in spots that have kept their original beauty.

o And that takes us to another major point in the article: the world under the sea. That's actually the main reason the Red Sea is so famous worldwide, isn't it?

o Exactly. That's the primary reason. The water there is unbelievably clear, which allows you to see coral reefs in all their colors, with their rich marine life. It's breathtaking. The reefs themselves are formed by tiny organisms that take thousands of years to grow into those structures.

o So is diving just about going under the water?

o Not at all. It's a whole different story. The article mentions spots like Ras Mohammed and the Giftun Islands—world-class diving sites.

o What makes them so special?

o The idea is that you enter another world—stunning coral colors, fascinating shapes, schools of colorful fish, and sometimes rare creatures.

o Like what, for example?

o Like giant sea turtles. And sometimes dolphins come and play around the boats. It's a full experience. The region is also important for migratory birds, with natural reserves both in the sea and on land.

o But with all that success and tourist expansion, surely there's another side to the story. The article mentioned environmental challenges, right?

o Of course. That's the flip side. The beautiful coral reefs we're talking about are also very fragile. The article points out practices that can damage them easily—for example, fishing or tourist boats dropping anchors carelessly. That can break corals that take years to grow.

o I see.

o Or oil and fuel leaks from the many boats—that pollutes the water.

o Did the article also mention other problems like excessive building or waste?

o Of course. Uncontrolled building—even organized, but too intense—puts pressure on the environment. And improper disposal of solid waste or sewage directly affects water clarity and marine life. All of this creates a negative environmental impact. Balancing the benefits of tourism with protecting the environment is a very tough equation.

o   So are there efforts to balance this out? Did the article say anything about that?

o   Yes, there are efforts. The article explained that there are many government and community initiatives—beach and seabed clean-up campaigns, and also training programs for workers in the tourism sector to learn how to operate in an eco-friendly way. The general trend now is toward sustainable tourism.

o   And what does that mean, simply put—"sustainable tourism"?

o   Very simply, it means we enjoy the beauty of the place and benefit from it economically, but without consuming or destroying it for future generations. It means finding ways for tourism to protect the environment and benefit local communities over the long term. There are regulations being set up, and attempts to monitor environmental impact.

o   But the challenge is always in applying and enforcing them.

o   Exactly. That's the real challenge.

o   So could we say the whole story revolves around the idea of balance?

o   That's the real conclusion. The Red Sea's success and appeal depend mainly on our ability to protect its treasures. It's not just about offering good hotels—the foundation is preserving the very nature that people travel from all over the world to see.

o   That makes you think: if a place's appeal is built entirely on its unique natural environment, how can it continue to attract people if that environment itself changes or disappears? And what would sustainable tourism really look like in such a vital area to ensure this beauty lasts? It's an important question that really needs thought.

Unit 10: Oases and Wonders

o   Today we're going to talk about places in Egypt that have a special magic—far away from the noise and crowds of the cities: the Egyptian oases.

o   Yes, the oases really are whole other worlds.

o   We read an article that described them as not just patches of greenery and water in the desert, but places with their own character, people, and history.

- o Exactly. The article gives a beautiful panorama of well-known oases like Siwa, Dakhla, Kharga, and also Farafra. Each one has its own story, its own details, completely different from the others.

- o Let's start with one that's maybe the most famous, or at least has a very distinctive character: Siwa.

- o Yes, Siwa.

- o It's way out west near Libya. The article focused on how its culture is different—they speak Amazigh as well as Arabic.

- o Right, that's a very important point. That cultural diversity is an essential part of Siwa's identity.

- o And then there are the monuments—like the Temple of Amun, Cleopatra's Spring, the salt lakes. And the houses—they're unusual, built from a material called karsheef. What's that?

- o Ah, karsheef is a story in itself. It's a local building material, a mix of salt, mud, and fine sand. The people there use the resources around them very cleverly to build houses that suit the climate and the environment.

- o Amazing. The article also mentioned that Siwa is famous for its olives and dates.

- o Very much so. Siwan olives and dates are some of the best, and they're the backbone of the small-scale local economy.

- o Okay, if we leave Siwa and head toward the New Valley, there's Dakhla and Kharga. The article says those are the most fertile.

- o Yes, it's different there. They're more like agricultural centers—broad, productive lands.

- o And you can even see that in the houses. The article described the mud-brick houses.

- o Exactly. Mud-brick houses aren't just a traditional look. They have a real function—the mud helps keep houses cool in summer and warm in winter. Natural air-conditioning, basically.

- o And with an artistic touch too—simple wall paintings.

- o Yes, simple, beautiful designs that reflect their environment. And Kharga also has administrative importance—it's the provincial capital, with Roman ruins and museums too.

- o Now to Farafra. The article described it as the smallest and quietest.

- o Yes, Farafra—it's really a place of calm. The population is small.

- And it's close to a place that looks almost surreal: the White Desert.

- Exactly. Being near the White Desert gives it a whole other dimension. And that brings us to the nature of life in the oases in general. The article emphasizes that life there has a different rhythm.

- A calm, simple rhythm.

- Yes. People are close to the land and water—farming is the foundation. Palms, olives, grains. What really struck me was the description of the irrigation system, the foggara. It seemed brilliant.

- It's brilliant and ingenious. The foggara is an ancient, precise engineering system—underground channels that bring water from faraway wells to the fields, minimizing evaporation.

- Wow. Using water wisely in such a tough environment—true wisdom.

- Yes, the wisdom of ancestors dealing with a difficult environment.

- Alright, that's farming and architecture. What about the people and their society? The article used the phrase "tight-knit community."

- And that's very accurate. The nature of the oasis brings people closer together. Relationships are strong—everyone knows everyone, and they help one another. A central value there is hospitality.

- Generosity, you mean.

- Exactly. Welcoming guests is sacred. The first thing you're offered is dates and tea—a genuine symbol of hospitality.

- Beautiful. And although technology has begun to reach them, the article says they still hold firmly to tradition.

- Definitely. That's very clear in many things—like their folk songs and dances, which appear at weddings or harvest season. Harvest time is a very important celebration.

- Does harvest season have its own rituals?

- Yes of course—celebrations, songs, giving thanks to the land for its bounty.

- And the beauty isn't just inside the oases themselves, but also in the surroundings. Like we said, the White Desert near Farafra. The article described its strange geological formations.

- Truly strange. The White Desert is like an open-air museum—white limestone rocks sculpted by the wind over thousands of years into surreal shapes: mushrooms, chickens, camels. The scene is dreamlike. The article also mentioned natural caves in the mountains near some oases, like

Dakhla, sometimes with ancient carvings and drawings telling the region's history.

o   Wow. And there's also something called quicksand, which sounds scary.

o   Not as terrifying as in the movies. It's just areas with very fine, loose sand. You just need to be careful walking there—and best to go with a local guide who knows the area well.

o   Got it. And the mountains themselves must be beautiful scenery.

o   Of course. The mountains surrounding the oases complete this stunning natural picture. So if we summarize what we got from the article: the Egyptian oases are a whole world of their own—breathtaking nature, ancient history still visible in monuments and systems like the foggara,

o   Yes—

o   And a simple, close-knit social life built on values like hospitality and cooperation. Plus the smart use of local resources—like mud-brick in Kharga and Dakhla, and karsheef in Siwa.

o   It's truly a unique and distinctive mix. And that makes us think about the future—with the rapid changes happening in the world and technology spreading more and more, how can the oases maintain that delicate balance?

o   A very important question.

o   How can they keep their magic, simplicity, and heritage, while also benefiting from development?

o   Yes, it's a difficult equation—balancing progress with preserving the identity and soul of the place.

o   Exactly. That's an open question—and maybe one worth each of us reflecting on.

Unit 11: Egypt's Official Governorates

o   Welcome! Today we're going to take a look at a really important topic that affects all of us in Egypt: the country's administrative divisions—how Egypt is divided today into 27 governorates, each with its own borders and system. And this idea itself is very old.

o   Of course, from the time of the Pharaohs and their provinces. Administrative division is absolutely essential, it's the framework the state uses to deliver services and manage resources everywhere. That's why it's important to understand how things work. That's what we'll try to chat about today, based on the article in front of us.

- So where do we start? With the most important figure in the governorate: the governor. This position is appointed by presidential decree, and it carries big responsibilities.

- Exactly. He's the one who supervises the implementation of government policies in practically everything—education, health, transport—inside his governorate. He's basically the government's representative there.

- And there are also the local councils, right?

- Yes, the local councils are supposed to be elected by the people.

- The central government in Cairo and the local authority—the governor and the councils? How does coordination work?

- There has to be coordination, of course, but sometimes things get a bit slow, or responsibilities overlap between a ministry and the governorate.

- And that can delay things.

- It can delay services or hold up projects. So balancing central authority with local flexibility is a constant challenge, honestly.

- Okay. But are all governorates basically the same?

- No, of course not. There are very clear differences. We can divide them into three main types.

- Like what?

- First type: urban governorates—Cairo, Alexandria, Giza. These are the huge cities. They're extremely crowded, with high population density, fast-paced life, and concentrated services and economic activities.

- But they must have their own problems.

- Of course—traffic congestion, pollution, and pressure on infrastructure.

- Right. And the second type?

- Rural governorates, mostly in the Delta and Upper Egypt, where agriculture is the backbone of life. Places like Menoufia, Fayoum, Sohag. Life is calmer there, and farming is the foundation.

- And the challenges are different.

- Yes, services may be less than in the big cities, and non-agricultural job opportunities are more limited.

- And the third type is the ones with a special nature—the border governorates.

- Exactly. Like Sinai, the Red Sea, Matrouh, and the New Valley. These areas are geographically huge, but the population is sparse and spread out. Here, there are totally different considerations: security, border protection, and the challenge of how to deliver services and infrastructure to scattered communities in deserts and remote areas.

- And these differences between rural and urban governorates create another major problem: internal migration.

- That's it. Lots of people, especially young people, leave their villages and head to the big cities.

- Looking for better opportunities.

- Yes, better jobs, education, and services. And this puts massive pressure on the cities, while the countryside risks losing its youth—the very foundation of its development.

- And this is linked to another serious problem: population distribution in Egypt.

- Exactly. More than 95% of Egyptians live in a very small strip along the Nile and Delta.

- Which creates unbelievable population density in that narrow strip.

- Exactly—pressure on everything: housing, transport, schools, hospitals, even water and land. Meanwhile, the vast majority of Egypt's land is almost empty, or very sparsely populated, and it needs a huge amount of work to attract people to live there.

- So, are there any solutions to these problems? Is the state trying to do anything?

- Of course, there are efforts. The biggest initiative right now is "Hayah Karima" (Decent Life).

- Yes, we hear a lot about it.

- It's truly a massive initiative. Its main goal is to develop Egyptian villages, especially the ones most in need, in rural governorates. The article points out the focus on infrastructure: sanitation, clean water, gas, electricity, plus schools and health units. It's basically an attempt to reduce the gap between rural and urban areas and encourage people to stay where they are.

- And technology plays a role in this too.

- Of course. Now they're using Geographic Information Systems (GIS)—advanced mapping tools that show exactly how people are distributed and what each area specifically needs in terms of services. That makes planning better and more accurate.

- Excellent. So, to summarize: Egypt has 27 governorates, each managed by a governor with local councils. They can be broadly classified as urban, rural, or border governorates. There are challenges like internal migration and uneven population distribution. But there are also major initiatives, like "Hayah Karima" and the use of technology, to help.

- Exactly. And the big question for the future is: what more can we do? How can local administration work better? How can we use technology more deeply to achieve greater balance among all governorates? And how can each region grow and serve its people better? That's a really important question—and one that needs serious thought.

Unit 12: Cultural and Informal Divisions

- Welcome everyone. Today we're going to talk about a really important topic for anyone living in Egypt—or anyone interested in it. We came across an article that caught our attention. It looks at how Egyptians themselves see their country, and how there are local divisions that feel very different from the official map we all know. We always hear people say Wagh Bahari and Wagh Qibli. But what's the real story behind these terms?

- Hello! Yes, this is a fascinating subject. The divisions you're talking about—the article calls them "popular divisions." They go much deeper than the administrative map of the 27 governorates.

- So it's not just the official governorates on paper?

- Exactly. These divisions are tied more closely to people's culture, their everyday language, the history of the region, and their sense of belonging. It's more about local identity. They're not just names of areas, but reflections of how people see themselves and the places they're connected to.

- Right, so there's a difference between the official administrative system and the way people themselves feel. Okay, to get a clearer picture—what are the differences between Wagh Bahari and Wagh Qibli?

- Well, this way of dividing Egypt is very old, deeply rooted in everyday speech and interactions. The word Baharimeans "towards the sea"—that is, the areas near the Mediterranean in the north.

- So, the north. Got it.

- Yes. This includes governorates like Alexandria, Beheira, Kafr El-Sheikh, and the Delta governorates such as Gharbia, and Monufia. These areas are known for their fertile farmland, high population density, and strong commercial and industrial activity, especially in the big cities.

- Okay, that covers the north. What about Qibli? The name itself is interesting.

- Yes—Qibli comes from the word qibla, meaning the direction of prayer, which points south. In Egypt, that term came to mean "the southern areas." So Wagh Qibli stretches roughly from Giza and Cairo down all the way to Aswan.

- So here, "upper" means "further south."

- Exactly. These governorates include Beni Suef, Minya, Assiut, Sohag, Qena, Luxor, and Aswan. The character of these regions is somewhat different.

- Different how?

- Many of them are more rural compared to the big northern cities. Agriculture is central, relying directly on the Nile. The region is known for crops like sugarcane and dates. And there's also a general perception that southern society is a bit more traditional or conservative compared to the north.

- So the differences aren't just in geography, crops, or population. You mentioned the social character—that must also show up in language and customs.

- Of course, of course. And maybe this is one of the clearest differences we can notice—the dialect. The dialect of Upper Egypt, the people of Wagh Qibli, has its own distinct sound, its own vocabulary and expressions that set it apart from the Cairo dialect. And this dialect is a really important part of their local identity, and they're very proud of it.

- True, true!

- And if you look at customs and traditions, you'll often find a stronger attachment to inherited practices in Wagh Qibli.

- Such as?

- It might show up in traditional clothing in some places, or in the ways of celebrating social occasions like weddings, or even in the nature of relationships between neighbors and people of the same area, which tend to be stronger.

- And in contrast, how does it look in Bahari?

- o In Bahari, especially in the big cities and in areas with more trade and industry, you often notice more flexibility in these customs, and more openness to outside influences. That's natural, given the higher movement of people and greater diversity in the cities there.

- o Right, I see.

- o Of course, that doesn't mean there are no traditions. There certainly are. But the way people hold onto them or express them can be a bit different. Each part of Egypt—whether Bahari or Qibli—has its own local identity.

- o Exactly, and that makes me think: Egyptian identity isn't one single, uniform thing. It's more like layers—there's the broad Egyptian identity that unites everyone, and beneath it are these local identities, each with its own traits and colors.

- o That's exactly it. And it's important to realize that identity isn't just lines on a map—it's feelings, history, and shared culture. What's beautiful is that despite all these differences—whether in dialect, traditions, lifestyle, or local identity—there's always a strong thread tying everyone together. And that thread is belonging to the nation.

- o Yes.

- o Love for Egypt, the bond with the Nile, and the shared history and heritage. That's what makes the Egyptian identity strong and united, despite its rich cultural diversity. And that unity always shows in important moments—whether in national celebrations or in times of challenge.

- o That's very true. And this leads us to a deeper question worth thinking about: how can this rich local diversity—these beautiful differences—continue to be a source of strength for the national Egyptian identity, rather than ever turning into a source of division? That's a point that really deserves reflection.

lingualism

Visit our website for information on current and upcoming titles and free language learning resources.

www.lingualism.com